The Admirable Crichton

A FANTASY IN FOUR ACTS

By J. M. Barrie

SAMUEL FRENCH, INC.

25 WEST 45TH STREET   NEW YORK 10036
7623 SUNSET BOULEVARD   HOLLYWOOD 90046
LONDON   *TORONTO*

THE ADMIRABLE CRICHTON

(5 Males; 6 Females)

STORY OF THE PLAY

One of the best known of Barrie's fantastic modern plays. Concerned with an aristocratic English family who revert to the state of Nature when shipwrecked on a desert island. While there they are willing slaves of their former butler, but on return to civilization the positions are shifted.

THE ADMIRABLE CRICHTON

Produced at the Duke of York's Theatre, London, on Tuesday, November 4th, 1902. The following is a list of the principal characters and the people who played them:

THE EARL OF LOAM .... *Mr. Henry Kemble*
HON. ERNEST WOOLLEY .... *Mr. Gerald Du Maurier*
REV. JOHN TREHERNE ...... *Mr. Clarence Blakiston*
LORD BROCKLEHURST .... *Mr. Carter Pickford*
A NAVAL OFFICER .... *Mr. J. C. Buckstone*
CRICHTON .... *Mr. H. B. Irving*
TOMPSETT .... *Mr. Compton Coutts*
LADY MARY LASENBY .... *Miss Irene Vanbrugh*
LADY CATHERINE LASENBY ...... *Miss Sybil Carlisle*
LADY AGATHA LASENBY ...... *Miss Muriel Beaumont*
COUNTESS OF BROCKLEHURST .. *Miss Fanny Coleman*
FISHER .... *Miss Margaret Fraser*
ELIZA ("TWEENY") .... *Miss Pattie Browne*

THE ADMIRABLE CRICHTON

Produced by Charles Frohman at the Lyceum Theatre, New York, November 17, 1903.

CAST

MR. CRICHTON .... *William Gillette*
HON. ERNEST WOOLLEY .... *Carter Pickford*
REV. JOHN TREHERNE .... *Harold Heaton*
LORD BROCKLEHURST .... *Soldene Powell*
FISHER .... *Sybil Campbell*
THE EARL OF LOAM .... *Henry Kemble*
NAVAL OFFICER .... *H. A. Morey*
TOMPSETT .... *Frederick Morris*
LADY MARY LASENBY .... *Sybil Carlisle*
TWEENY .... *Pattie Brown*
LADY CATHERINE LASENBY .... *Beatrice Irwin*
LADY AGATHA LASENBY .... *Rosalind Coghlan*
COUNTESS OF BROCKLEHURST .... *Kate Meek*
SERVANTS *at the* EARL OF LOAM'S:
    Maud Giroux, Charles S. Marshall, Fred Court-
    eney, Florence L. Busby, Evelyn Harris, Ernest
    Crawford, Archie Fahnestock, Frances Comstock,
    Florence Honey, Joseph F. Moreland, Ethel Bruce
    and Arthur Willmore.

The Admirable Crichton

ACT I

SCENE: *The scene is a drawing-room in the* EARL OF
LOAM'S *house in Mayfair. It is about 4 p.m. in
summer.*

*(A Ground Plan will be found of each scene at
the end of the book.)*

*A full description of the furniture and properties
will be found in the Property Plot, but the chief
features are as follows:*

The doors are at the back. Double doors L.C.
leading to the hall. A single door R.C. *to other
rooms. Windows in the* L. *wall. The fireplace in the*
R. *wall. At* R.C., *and down* L.C., *are settees. Up* L.C.,
*an oval table with a tray and tea-things for about
eighteen persons. On the* R. *of this table, an armchair with rather a tall back. At the* L. *end of the
settee* R.C., *a small round table, with stools above
and below it, and a chair to the* L. *of it. Chairs
above and below the fireplace, and at the windows.
A large bookcase up* L., *and a glass-fronted china-
cabinet up* C., *between the two doors.*

*The furniture is so adjusted that both settees
and almost every chair and stool, can be occupied
without any character being masked.*

*The furniture and the décor generally is Ed-
wardian, or very late Victorian with a few well-
blended additions of the former period.*

As the CURTAIN *rises,* CRICHTON, *the butler,
ushers in the* HON. ERNEST WOOLLEY. CRICHTON
is the beau ideal of a butler in a correct establish-

ment. There has never been quite such a perfect butler. He is also an excellent fellow who has achieved greatness in his calling because he thinks it a truly noble one. When agitated, he rubs his hands together a trifle servilely, but at all other times he is dignity personified. His age is about thirty-five.

ERNEST is fresh from Oxford and has the complaisant manner of one who knows pretty well everything. He enjoys his gift of epigrammatic conversation.

CRICHTON enters up L.C. and stands C. as ERNEST enters and comes down C., then to below the armchair L.C., and surveys the tea-table. As he speaks, CRICHTON goes up, closes the doors, and turns to cross R.

ERNEST. I perceive, Crichton, from the teacups, that the *great* function is to take place here.

CRICHTON (*whom the matter referred to evidently depresses*). Yes, sir.

(He is going R., but when ERNEST speaks he stops C.)

ERNEST. The servants' hall coming up to have tea in the drawing-room—no wonder you look happy, Crichton.

CRICHTON (*miserably*). No, sir.

ERNEST (*looking at him*). Do you know, Crichton, I think that with an effort you might look even happier. (*He sits in the armchair L.C. CRICHTON makes the action with his hands and tries to smile.*) You don't approve of his lordship's compelling his servants to be his equals—once a month?

CRICHTON (*moving down to R. of the chair L.C.*). It is not for me, sir, to disapprove of his lordship's radical views.

ERNEST. Certainly not. And it's only once a month that he is affable to you, Crichton.

CRICHTON. On all other days of the month, sir, his lordship's treatment of us is—everything that could be desired.

ERNEST *(lifting a cup)*. Teacups! Life, Crichton, is like a cup of tea, the more heartily we drink, the sooner we reach the dregs. Ha, ha! *(He smiles, pleased with his epigram, and looks at* CRICHTON *to see how it has impressed him.)*

CRICHTON *(repeats the action with his hands and smiles servilely)*. Thank you, sir.

ERNEST *(rather confidentially, putting down the cup and rising)*. Crichton, in case I should be asked to say a few words to the servants, I have strung together a little speech. *(Coming down* C. *a pace, looking about. His hand strays to his pocket—he smiles like one who knows what an uncommon good speech it is.)* I was wondering where I could stand. *(He leans over the back of the high chair* L.C. *like one addressing an audience.)* Yes, here.

(CRICHTON *looks from him to the chair and evidently feels that the chair is too high, crosses for a hassock* R. *and puts it behind the* L.C. *chair for* ERNEST *to stand on, then he exits majestically* R.C. ERNEST, *however, is annoyed, and stares after him. He kicks the hassock* R., *then again tries the position.)*

ERNEST *(addressing an imaginary audience)*. Suppose you were all little fishes at the bottom of the sea. *(He smiles, well pleased.)* And suppose—— *(He is not quite satisfied with his position; evidently feels he is a little short. He looks at the hassock, crosses* R. *and lifts it when—)*

(Enter up L.C., LADY AGATHA LASENBY, *followed by* LADY CATHERINE LASENBY. *They are lazy, fashionable girls.* ERNEST *is caught with the hassock and affects jocularity, backing down* R.C.)

ERNEST (*hiding the hassock behind him*). And how are my little friends to-day?

(*They see the hassock and look at each other inquiringly.*)

LADY AGATHA (*crossing to L. and shaking her head at him*). Don't be silly, Ernest. (*Crossing to L. and throwing herself on the settee.*) If you want to know how we are, we are dead. Even to think of entertaining the servants is so exhausting.

ERNEST (*moving towards the settee L.C.*). Poor ickle sing! Then why do you do it?

LADY CATHERINE (*moving down L. of the settee R.C.*). Why? Because Father compels us. You know what Father is when he takes up an idea.

ERNEST (*turning to her*). I have noticed that the stouter he grows, the fuller he is of ideas.

(LADY CATHERINE *moves down* R.)

LADY AGATHA. This is his most horrid one. He holds, Ernest—he read it somewhere—that servants are our brothers and sisters, and have hearts and minds and souls just like ours.

ERNEST. I say, he *is* getting stout!

LADY CATHERINE (*turning to* R.). And he insists that it is his solemn duty, as a peer of the realm, to elevate and ennoble our servants, and that the best way of doing this is to treat them as our equals—not every day, you know, but once a month.

LADY AGATHA. Yes, once a month we are compelled to receive them here in the drawing-room and chat with them on equal terms and hand them tea and cake—in order to elevate them.

ERNEST. What a joke!

LADY CATHERINE. Joke! It's awful! I'm sure they loathe it, but Father says it brings the time nearer when man and man "shall brothers be for all that."

ERNEST. And this is the day when you have to hand round the tea!

LADY AGATHA. It so exhausts me.

(LADY CATHERINE *sits on the chair down* R.)

ERNEST *(moving* C. *and looking from one to the other).* You poor overworked things—— *(He crosses to* L.C.) Rest your weary limbs.

LADY CATHERINE. But why have you a hassock in your hand?

LADY AGATHA. Yes.

ERNEST. Why! *(He looks at the hassock and conceives an excuse.)* You see, as the servants are to be the guests, I must be the butler, I was practising. This is a tray—observe—— *(Holding the hassock like a tray, he goes mincingly from* L. *to* R. *in waiter fashion.)*

(Enter LADY MARY LASENBY R. *She is the eldest and laziest of the girls, haughty and rather indolent in an aristocratic way. As* LADY MARY *comes down* C., ERNEST, *at* R., *turns and faces her with the hassock.)*

ERNEST. Tea, my lady?

LADY MARY *(with insolent hauteur).* It's only *you,* Ernest—— *(She crosses and sits on the settee* R.) I thought there was someone here.

(LADY AGATHA *shows indignation at the remark.)*

ERNEST *(annoyed, throwing down the hassock, on which* LADY CATHERINE *puts her foot).* So I'm nobody, am I? *(He changes to sarcasm as he sees her reclining.)* Had a very tiring day, also, Mary?

LADY MARY. Dreadfully! (ERNEST *arranges the cushions for her comfort.)* I've been trying on engagement rings all morning.

ERNEST *(excited)*. Eh—what's that! *(Crossing to* LADY AGATHA.*)* Is it Brocklehurst? *(*LADY AGATHA *nods—*ERNEST *turns to* LADY MARY, *crossing up above the* R. *settee.)* You have given your warm young heart to Brocky? *(*LADY MARY *doesn't bother to answer.* ERNEST *leans over the settee.* LADY MARY *turns her head away.)* I don't wish to fatigue you, Mary, by insisting on a verbal answer, but if, without straining yourself, you could signify Yes or No—— Won't you make the effort? *(*LADY MARY *lazily holds up her left hand on which is a ring.* ERNEST *takes hold of her hand.)* The ring! *(He tragically puts his hand to his heart.)* Then I am too late. *(He crosses to* C., *and repeats like an operatic villain.)* "I am too late." *(He moves down* C., *stops suddenly, and turns to* LADY MARY.*)* May I ask, Mary, does Brocky know? *(*LADY CATHERINE *and* LADY AGATHA *close their eyes.* LADY MARY *looks indignant and then closes her eyes also.)* I mean—of course, it was that terrible mother of his that pulled this through—mother does everything for Brocky. Still, in the eyes of the law—you will not be her wife, but his—and therefore I hold that Brocky ought to be informed. Now—— *(He looks at her, sees she has got her eyes closed, then looks at the* OTHERS, *who have also got their eyes closed.)* If you girls are shamming sleep in the expectation that I shall awaken you in the manner beloved of ladies, abandon all such hopes.

*(*LADY CATHERINE *and* LADY AGATHA *look up.)*

LADY MARY *(speaking without looking up)*. You impertinent boy!

ERNEST. I knew that was it, though I didn't know everything, Agatha. *(With a clever air.)* I'm not young enough to know everything. *(He looks from one to the other to see the effect of his epigram.)*

(A pause, in which they all three look at one another.)

LADY AGATHA *(the only person who really admires* ERNEST'S *brilliancy). Young* enough?

ERNEST. Don't you see? I'm not young enough to know everything.

LADY AGATHA. I'm sure it's frightfully clever, but it's so puzzling.

(Opening the doors up L.C., CRICHTON *ushers in the* REV. JOHN TREHERNE, *an athletic, pleasant-faced clergyman.)*

CRICHTON. Mr. Treherne.

(Coming down C., TREHERNE *bows to* AGATHA *and crosses* R., *to* LADY CATHERINE. CRICHTON *then crosses to above the tea-table up* L. *after closing the doors.)*

LADY CATHERINE. Ernest, say it to Mr. Treherne.

*(*TREHERNE, *after greeting* CATHERINE, *turns to* LADY MARY.*)*

ERNEST. Look here, Treherne, I'm not young enough to know everything.

TREHERNE *(having shaken hands with* LADY MARY*).* How do you mean, old chap?

ERNEST *(tartly).* I mean what I say.

LADY MARY. Say it again—say it more slowly.

ERNEST.   I'm—not—young—enough—to—know— everything.

TREHERNE *(standing at* R., *with his back to the fire-place).* I see. What you really mean, my boy, is that you are not *old enough* to know everything.

ERNEST. No, I don't.

TREHERNE. I assure you, that's it.

LADY MARY. Of course it is.

ALL. Yes, Ernest, that's it.

ERNEST *(to* CRICHTON*).* Crichton! (CRICHTON

comes from above the table L.C. *to the* R. *of* ERNEST.)
I am not young enough, Crichton, to know everything.
Ha, ha!

(A pause. CRICHTON *repeats the hand business—then
smiles.* ERNEST *smiles to encourage him.)*

CRICHTON. Thank you, sir.

(He turns and exits L.C., *closing the doors.)*

ERNEST *(triumphant).* Ah, if you had that fellow's
head, Treherne, you would find something better to do
with it than play cricket. I hear you bowl with your
head. *(He moves a little down* L.C.)
TREHERNE *(good-humouredly, moving towards* C.).
I'm afraid cricket is all I'm good for, Ernest.
LADY CATHERINE *(who admires him).* Indeed, it
isn't. You are sure to get on, Mr. Treherne.
TREHERNE *(crossing down* C.). Thank you, Lady
Catherine.
LADY CATHERINE. But it was the Bishop who told
me so. He said a *clergyman* with a *leg break* was sure
to get on in England.
TREHERNE. I'm jolly glad. *(He moves down* R.C.,
towards her.)

(Enter up L.C., LORD BROCKLEHURST, *preceded by*
LORD LOAM. LORD LOAM *is pompous and fussy.*
LORD BROCKLEHURST *is a starchy, correct young
man.* BROCKLEHURST *crosses to the back of the
settee* R. *and shakes hands with* LADY MARY.)

LORD LOAM *(crossing down and shaking hands with*
ERNEST). You are here, Ernest. *(He shakes hands with*
TREHERNE, *who has crossed up to him.)* Feeling fit for
the voyage, Treherne?
TREHERNE. Looking forward to it enormously. *(He*

turns up above the R. *settee, and shakes hands with*
LORD BROCKLEHURST.)

LORD LOAM. That's right. *(He crosses to* R.) Now
then, Mary, up and doing, up and doing. Time we had
the servants in, *(he rings the bell at the fireplace)* they
enjoy it so much.

(LADY CATHERINE *rises, crosses up* C., *is joined by*
TREHERNE *and they go to the table* L.C. LADY
AGATHA *rises, throws down the cushion, and goes
to* L. *of the table* L.C.)

LADY MARY *(rises)*. They hate it.
LORD LOAM. Mary, to your duties.

(LADY MARY *crosses up to below the table* L.C. LORD
BROCKLEHURST *comes down* C. ERNEST *moves toward him.)*

ERNEST. (L. *of* LORD BROCKLEHURST). Congratula-
tions, Brocky.
LORD BROCKLEHURST *(stiffly)*. Thanks.
ERNEST. Mother's pleased?
LORD BROCKLEHURST *(with dignity)*. Mother is *very*
pleased.
ERNEST. That's good. Do you go on the yacht with
us?
LORD BROCKLEHURST. Sorry, can't. And look here,
Ernest, I will *not* be called Brocky.
ERNEST. Mother don't like it?
LORD BROCKLEHURST. She does not. *(He crosses
down* L. *below the* L. *settee and sits.)*

(LADY MARY, *coming to above the* L. *settee, speaks to*
LORD BROCKLEHURST. ERNEST *crosses down* R.
below the fireplace, and stands on the hassock. Two
FOOTMEN *outside open the doors for* CRICHTON
and are seen by the audience. Enter CRICHTON

with a tea-pot on a tray, he comes below the arm-chair L.C. *and puts the teapot on the table and remains, below the armchair* L.C.)

LORD LOAM *(crossing to* C., *genially).* We are quite ready, Crichton.

(CRICHTON *is reluctant and distressed.)*

LADY MARY *(sarcastically).* How he enjoys it!
LORD LOAM *(angrily).* He is the only one who doesn't —pitiful creature!

(The OTHERS *are all smiling at this.)*

CRICHTON *(humbly).* I can't help being a Conservative, my lord.
LORD LOAM. Be a man, Crichton. You are the same flesh and blood as myself.
CRICHTON *(rubbing his hands in pain).* Oh, my lord.
LORD LOAM *(sharply).* Show them in, and, by the way, they were not all here last time.
CRICHTON. All, my lord, except the merest trifles.
LORD LOAM. It must be every one. *(Threateningly.)* And remember this, Crichton—for the time being you are my equal. *(Firmly.)* I shall soon show you whether you are not my equal. Do as you are told. (CRICHTON *bows, goes up* C., *and exits, closing the doors, taking the tray with him.)* And girls— *(The girls look at him.)* Remember, no condescension. The first who condescends, recites. (LADY AGATHA, LADY CATHERINE *and* LADY MARY *resent the reference to recitation. They hastily busy themselves with preparations for tea.)* By the way, Brocklehurst, can you do anything?
LORD BROCKLEHURST. How do you mean?
LORD LOAM. Can you do anything—with a penny or a handkerchief, make them disappear, for instance?

(ERNEST *here tries to do a trick with a penny and his handkerchief.)*

LORD BROCKLEHURST. Good heavens, no.

LORD LOAM. It's a pity. Everyone in our position ought to be able to do something of that sort. Ernest, I shall probably ask you to say a few words—something bright and sparkling.

ERNEST. But, my dear Uncle, I have prepared nothing.

LORD LOAM. Anything impromptu will do. *(He moves up* R.C. *and surveys everything with satisfaction.)*

ERNEST *(moving towards* C.). Oh—well—if anything strikes me on the spur of the moment—— *(Craftily gets the hassock into position by giving it little kicks—to behind the chair* L.C. *and stands there for a moment.)*

LORD BROCKLEHURST. But what is going to happen? I feel alarmed!

(ERNEST *moves* L. *below the table to above the* L. *settee.)*

LORD LOAM *(coming down* C.). It is simply this, my dear Brocklehurst—I am a man, as you know, who despises class distinction, and I prove it by having all my servants up here to tea once a month. While they are here we treat them precisely as any other guest would be treated; and as this month's meeting happens to be to-day, you will have an opportunity of seeing how it delights and elevates them. *(He moves a little down* R.C., *rubbing his hands.)*

(CRICHTON *enters* L.C. *The doors remain open. He stands* C., *and announces the servants.* LORD BROCKLEHURST *rises, standing down* L. MRS. PERKINS, *the housekeeper, enters and comes down* C.)

CRICHTON *(depressed but respectfully)*. Mrs. Perkins.

(LADY MARY *is preparing tea, the others are looking
after the cakes, etc., a busy group, above and to* L.
of the table.)

LORD LOAM (*shaking hands with* MRS. PERKINS).
Very delighted, Mrs. Perkins. (*He brings her down a
little, glaring at* LADY MARY.) Mary! (LADY MARY
gives a start.) Our friend, Mrs. Perkins.

(LADY MARY *crosses below the table to* MRS. PERKINS,
shakes hands and indicates the settee L.)

LADY MARY. Won't you sit here? (*She crosses up* C.
and turns to the tea-table.)
LORD LOAM. Agatha! (LADY AGATHA *comes forward, shakes hands and points to the settee* L., *crosses
and goes to* LADY MARY *for a cup of tea.* ERNEST, *who
is* L., *shakes hands with* MRS. PERKINS *and moves to
below the armchair* L.C., *as* MRS. PERKINS *goes to the*
L. *settee and sits at the* R. *end.*) Lord Brocklehurst, my
valued friend, Mrs. Perkins.

(LORD BROCKLEHURST *bows to* MRS. PERKINS, *who
rises, bows and sits again.* LADY CATHERINE
crosses down R. *of the settee and shakes hands
with* MRS. PERKINS. LADY CATHERINE *hands her
cake and then returns to the table* L. LADY AGATHA
hands her tea, over the back of the settee. LORD
LOAM *breaks a little* R.C., *and turns.*)

LORD BROCKLEHURST (*moving up* C., *to* L *of* ERN-
EST). For Heaven's sake, Ernest, don't leave me for a
moment, this sort of thing is *utterly* opposed to *all* my
principles.
ERNEST. You stick to me, Brocky, and I'll pull you
through.
CRICHTON. Monsieur Fleury.

(MONSIEUR FLEURY, *the French cook, enters.*)

ERNEST. The chef.

(LORD BROCKLEHURST *throws up his hands in disgust and crosses to the fireplace.* FLEURY *comes down* C.)

LORD LOAM *(moving to* C., *and shaking hands with the chef.)* Very charmed to see you, Monsieur Fleury.
FLEURY. Thank you very much. *(He bows to the ladies.)*
LORD LOAM *(glaring).* Agatha. (LADY AGATHA *tosses her head impatiently.)* Recitation!

(LADY AGATHA *gets a cup of tea, crosses and stands by* FLEURY. LORD LOAM, *unseen by the latter, makes another threatening gesture.* LADY AGATHA *holds out her hand, which* FLEURY *takes.)*

LADY AGATHA. How do you do? *(She takes him to the armchair down* R.)

(LORD BROCKLEHURST *turns up* R. *to the* R. *settee as* TREHERNE *crosses down* R. *and offers cake to* FLEURY.)

TREHERNE. And how's the weather using you?

(LADY AGATHA *gives* FLEURY *his cup and returns to* L. *of* LADY MARY *again.* TREHENE *stands talking to* FLEURY, *down* R.)

CRICHTON. Mr. Rolleston!

(MR. ROLLESTON *enters. He is a valet.* LORD BROCKLE-HURST *moves* R.C. *above the settee.)*

LORD LOAM *(shaking hands).* How do you do, Rolleston? (ROLLESTON *stands uneasily, turns and bows*

to the LADIES. LORD LOAM *indicates the chair above the
fireplace.* ROLLESTON *crosses and stands below it.*
TREHERNE *crosses up and talks to him, offering him
some cake. After watching* ROLLESTON, *calls* ERNEST,
who is just getting a cup of tea for ROLLESTON.)
Ernest! (ERNEST, *carrying the cup, crosses to him.*) I
can't understand how Rolleston manages to wear my
clothes.

(ERNEST *takes tea to* ROLLESTON *and then returns to
below the* R. *settee.*)

CRICHTON. Mr. Tompsett.
LADY MARY (*on the announcement of* MR. TOMP-
SETT). Ah, here's old Tompsett!

(MR. TOMPSETT *enters with his hat in his right hand.*
LORD LOAM *is about to shake it in mistake, when*
TOMPSETT *puts it in the other hand.*)

LORD LOAM. How do you do, Tompsett!

(LADY MARY *hands tea for* TOMPSETT *to* LADY
AGATHA.)

LADY CATHERINE (*crosses down to the lower end of
the settee* L. *and indicating the place*). How are you,
Tompsett; come and sit here.

(TOMPSETT *crosses down, touches his forehead to the
ladies and shakes hands with* MRS. PERKINS, *puts
his hat and gloves under the settee, sits down and
takes tea, etc.* LADY CATHERINE *and* LADY AGATHA
return to the table.)

CRICHTON. Miss Fisher!

(MISS FISHER *enters haughtily.* LORD LOAM, *who has*

crossed to below the armchair L.C., *turns and shakes hands.)*

LORD LOAM (L. *of* FISHER). How do you do, Miss Fisher?

(FISHER *just notices the ladies, who on the other hand, all notice the way her hair is dressed, and remark audibly upon it.)*

ERNEST *(coming forward).* This is a pleasure, Miss Fisher.

(He escorts her down R. FLEURY *rises and offers her the chair, and they stand talking to her.)*

CRICHTON. Miss Simmons.

(MISS SIMMONS *enters.* LORD LOAM *turns from* FISHER *to* C.)

LORD LOAM *(on her* R., *shaking hands).* You are always welcome, Miss Simmons. *(He passes her across to his* R.)
ERNEST *(crossing and shaking hands with* SIM-MONS). At last we meet. Won't you sit down?

(He takes her to the settee. SIMMONS *sits at the* R. *end,* ERNEST *talking to her.* TREHERNE *here crosses to the table* L.C. *for tea, and puts his plate on the table.)*

CRICHTON. Mademoiselle Jeanne.

(MADEMOISELLE JEANNE *enters and comes down* L. *of* LORD LOAM.)

LORD LOAM *(shaking hands).* Charmed to see you, Mademoiselle Jeanne.

(TREHERNE turns, shakes hands with JEANNE and crosses with FISHER'S tea down R. ERNEST rises, comes forward, shakes hands with JEANNE and takes her to the chair L. of the R. settee. LORD LOAM moves to below the armchair L.C. The conversation has now become general. LADY MARY rises and crosses down R.C. LADY CATHERINE follows LADY MARY to R., offers cake to FISHER and then to ROLLESTON and SIMMONS, during the following dialogue.)

LADY MARY *(during the above)* Your tea is coming, Jeanne. Your tea is coming, Simmons. Ah—Mr. Treherne, this is Fisher, my maid.

LORD LOAM *(sharply, taking a pace to C.)* Your what, Mary?

LADY MARY *(with an effort).* My friends.

(She then goes up to R., asking ROLLESTON and SIMMONS if they have all they want. Then to LORD BROCKLEHURST, exchanging inaudible expostulations, then to JEANNE and finally to the table L.C., followed by LORD BROCKLEHURST.)

CRICHTON. Thomas!

(Enter THOMAS, a footman. LORD LOAM crosses up and shakes hands with him.)

LORD LOAM (L. *of* THOMAS). How do you do, Thomas?

(THOMAS gives his hand reluctantly, bows to the ladies and crosses R.C.)

ERNEST *(rising and shaking hands).* How are you, Thomas?

(THOMAS moves R.)

CRICHTON. John.

(Enter JOHN, *another footman, who also comes down*
C.)

LORD LOAM (L. *of* JOHN, *shaking hands*). How do
you do, John?

(JOHN *breaks* R.C. *to* THOMAS *and* ERNEST. LORD LOAM
crosses down to TOMPSETT *and* MRS. PERKINS L.,
*who both rise, but he makes them sit again and
helps them to another cup of tea, which* LADY
MARY *makes, and after talking a little while, moves
to the chair* L.C. ERNEST *shakes hands with* JOHN
and calls LORD BROCKLEHURST, *who is up* L.C.)

ERNEST *(breaking to* L. *of* JOHN). Brocklehurst!
(LORD BROCKLEHURST *crosses down to him.*) This is
John. I think you have already met on the doorstep.
(He slaps LORD BROCKLEHURST *on the back and pushes
him towards* JOHN *and turns up* R.C., *talking to* JEANNE
above her chair.)

(LORD BROCKLEHURST, *annoyed, shakes hands with*
JOHN, *then crosses* L., *below the table and down to
the window* L. THOMAS *joins* JOHN R.C., *below the*
R. *end of the settee.* LORD LOAM, *noticing they have
nothing, call out.*)

LORD LOAM. Agatha! Catherine!

(They immediately take them tea and cake. THOMAS
takes his cup R. *to the fireplace.* LADY CATHERINE
remains up R.C. *between them, and* LADY AGATHA
returns to her place again. LADY CATHERINE *indicates the* L. *end of the* R. *settee, and* JOHN *sits, a
little reluctantly.*)

CRICHTON. Jane.

(JANE *enters shyly, stands up* C. CRICHTON *indicates*
LORD LOAM. LADY CATHERINE *moves down* R. *to*
TREHERNE. THOMAS *having moved up above the*
R. *end of the* R. *settee.*)

LORD LOAM *(holding out his hand).* Jane!

(JANE *crosses down and gives her hand, then stands
there until* TREHERNE *crosses, takes her hand and
escorts her to the chair above the fireplace, round
in front of the settee* R.C. TREHERNE *crosses to the
table* L.C. *for tea and returns to* JANE. LADY CATH-
ERINE *meanwhile crosses to her with cake.*)

CRICHTON. Gladys.

(GLADYS *enters, hanging her head shyly.* ERNEST *rises
and leaves* JEANNE.)

ERNEST *(coming down to* R. *of* GLADYS *and shaking
hands. She curtseys.)* How do you do, Gladys. You
know my uncle?

(GLADYS *shakes her head and sidles down.* ERNEST
turns and crosses to above the L. *end of the settee,
engaging* JOHN *and* JEANNE.)

LORD LOAM *(holding out his hand).* Your hand,
Gladys? *(He looks at* LADY AGATHA, *who is doing nothing.)* Agatha!

(LADY AGATHA *starts, crosses to* C., *gives her hand to*
GLADYS, *who is biting her handkerchief, takes it
awkwardly, and indicates the chair below the window down* L. GLADYS *crosses* L. LADY AGATHA
gets her some tea. LORD BROCKLEHURST *turns and
sees* GLADYS *and crosses up* L. *in horror and remains well up.* LADY AGATHA *takes the tea down to*
GLADYS. *During this* JOHN *has risen from the* R,

settee, crossed to FLEURY *and then to the* R. *end of the settee* R. *and is talking to* THOMAS. LORD LOAM *crosses and says a word or two to* FISHER *and returns to* L.C. *again.)*

CRICHTON. Eliza.

(ELIZA, *the "Tweeny," enters, frightened, with eyes on* CRICHTON *and, backing, falls into* LORD BROCK-LEHURST, *who is crossing from up* L. *Turning, she then backs down* C., *stumbles over the hassock, and stops* C.)

LORD LOAM *(on her* L., *giving her his hand.)* So happy to see you, Eliza. (ELIZA *turns and takes his hand and bobs.* LORD LOAM *turns and talks to* MRS. PERKINS. ELIZA *looks round frightened, bobs to* SIMMONS *and* FISHER, *then turns and bobs to the* LADIES. LORD BROCKLEHURST *crosses from the table with a plate of cake for* LADY CATHERINE *up* R.C. FISHER *gives her cup to* FLEURY, *which he puts down.* LORD LOAM *turns and sees* ELIZA, *still standing* C., *distressed.)* Don't be afraid, Eliza.

(LADY CATHERINE *crosses below the* R. *settee to* GLADYS *and hands her some cake after having taken the plate from* LORD BROCKLEHURST *and then returns to the tea-table* L.C.)

FISHER *(calling to* JOHN). John! *(He comes to her.)* I saw you talking to Lord Brocklehurst just now, introduce me. *(She rises and tidies herself.)*

(LORD LOAM *turns and gives more tea to* TOMPSETT *and* MRS. PERKINS.)

LORD BROCKLEHURST. That's an uncommon pretty girl. If I must feed one of them, Ernest, that's the one. *(He moves down,* L. *of the* R. *settee.)*

JOHN *(advancing and introducing* FISHER*).* My lord——

(But ERNEST *has followed* LORD BROCKLEHURST, *who is about to bow when* ERNEST *catches him by the arm and stops the introduction.)*

ERNEST. No, it won't do, you are too pretty, my dear! *(*FISHER *is at first offended. Then she smirks.* JOHN *crosses* R., *to* ROLLESTON.*)* Mother wouldn't like it. *(He turns and sees* ELIZA *who is watching them open-mouthed.)* Here's something safer. *(He draws* ELIZA *towards* LORD BROCKLEHURST R.C. *To* LORD BROCKLE-HURST.*)* Charming girl, dying to know you, let me introduce you, Eliza, Lord Brocklehurst—Lord Brock-lehurst, Eliza.

*(*LORD LOAM *now crosses up* C., *and above the table* L.C. *as* LORD BROCKLEHURST *turns, sees* ELIZA, *and after a first horrified look, bows and indicates the* R. *settee.* ELIZA *bobs to him, crosses him to the settee, and sits on the* L. *end. From either side of her* JEANNE *and* SIMMONS *regard her with disdain.* LORD BROCKLEHURST *crosses* L.C. *for tea and cake, returning with it to the settee. He bows to* SIM-MONS, *who is sitting at the* R. *end, and then sits in the centre of the settee, watching* ELIZA. *She takes a very large piece of cake and her cup. During this there has been a little movement generally, the* GIRLS *inquiring from various* SERVANTS *if they want more tea,* ERNEST *has gone down* R. *to talk to* FISHER, *and* LADY MARY *has seated herself in the armchair* L.C. *Much of this occurs simultaneously and only occupies a few moments.)*

LORD LOAM *(looking round).* They are not all here, Crichton.

*(*CRICHTON *crosses to the doors up* L.C., *and opens them.)*

CRICHTON (*calling off, facing* R.). Odds and ends!

(*He returns to his position up* C., *facing down. The remaining introductions are got through more quickly.* LORD LOAM *has crossed to* C., *and stands below and to* R. *of* CRICHTON, *facing* L. *The* STABLE BOY *enters, comes down and touches his forehead before taking* LORD LOAM'S *hand and shaking it. For want of something better,* LORD LOAM *laughs. The* STABLE BOY *backs a pace and bumps into* LADY MARY'S *chair. She and* LADY AGATHA *give a little cry, and the former rises, very annoyed. The* STABLE BOY *backs away from her, touching his forehead again to her and* LORD LOAM, *who indicates to* LADY MARY *that she must shake hands. She moves to him and does so, then indicating the stool* R. *of the* L. *settee. The* STABLE BOY *crosses to it and sits.* LADY MARY *flips her fingers, as a sign to* LADY AGATHA *to attend to his tea.* LADY AGATHA *rushes* LADY CATHERINE *up to the table and the three argue quietly but excitedly as to which is to give the boy his tea.* LORD LOAM, *seeing this, crosses to the table and bends over it, speaking threateningly.)*

LORD LOAM. Which is to recite? (*They* ALL *look at him for a moment, then each take a cup of tea to the* STABLE BOY. *He takes* LADY MARY'S *and the others put theirs down and bring him cake.* LADY MARY *returns to and sits in the armchair* L.C. *as a* KITCHEN WENCH *enters, clasping her hands behind her as she comes down.* LORD LOAM, *down* C., *offers her his hand.)* How do you do, my friend? (*The* KITCHEN WENCH *brings her right arm up from behind her like a semaphore, just touches his hand and puts her own arm behind her again, at the same time bobbing.)* Catherine! (LADY CATHERINE *looks up from* L. *of the table, sees what he means, seizes a plate of biscuits and goes below the table to* L. *of the* KITCHEN WENCH *and offers her hand. The* KITCHEN WENCH *bobs, and repeats the arm business.* LADY CATHERINE *indicates the chair* L. *between the windows, as* LADY AGATHA, *above the table, takes a cup to* LADY MARY *to fill with tea. The* KITCHEN WENCH *moves to below and* R. *of* LADY MARY'S *chair, and shoots her arm out again almost in* LADY MARY'S *face.* LADY MARY *gives a startled cry, jerking the cup, and looks up at the* KITCHEN WENCH, *who goes to below table, repeats the arm business to* LADY AGATHA, *bobs, and crosses to the chair between the windows and sinks into it. After an exchange of despairing glances,* LADY AGATHA *takes the cup from* LADY MARY *to the* KITCHEN WENCH. LADY CATHERINE *moves up* R. *of the table to above it, and* LADY AGATHA *then joins her. A* PAGE BOY *has now entered, looking at* CRICHTON *for guidance, who points out* LORD LOAM. *The* PAGE BOY *comes down and* LORD LOAM *offers his hand. The* PAGE BOY *looks again at* CRICHTON *before shaking hands.)* Why, you're getting quite a big boy. *(He pats the* PAGE BOY *on the head and passes him across to* R. TREHERNE, *who is sitting on the stool above the table* L. *of the* R. *settee, indicates the stool below it, and the* PAGE BOY *sits. At the same time,* LADY MARY *rises and moves to* L. *of the tea-table and* LORD LOAM *moves a little* L.C., *below the armchair. The* PAGE BOY, *sitting, sees* ELIZA *and nods to her. At the same time* LADY CATHERINE *crosses above the table and down to him, with tea and cake. The* PAGE BOY *rises, but she makes him sit again, and take the tea. She then turns up* L. *of the* R. *settee and to* L. *of* TREHERNE. *The* PAGE BOY *puts his cake on the floor, finding things a bit awkward. He then pours the tea into his saucer as it is too hot, puts the cup on the floor and drinks.* CRICHTON *has now closed the doors and returned to his place. During the above,* LORD LOAM *goes up to the table fussing about.)* Keep it going— keep it going— *(He turns to face* R., *as* LADY CATHERINE *returns from* TREHERNE *with the cakeplate.)* Who is this for?

LADY CATHERINE. The coachman.

LORD LOAM *(taking the plate)*. I shall give it to him. *(He goes down to the L. settee.)* Cake, Tompsett?

TOMPSETT *(rising and taking cake)*. Thank you, my lord.

(During this, LADY CATHERINE has returned to TREHERNE above the L. end of the R. settee. LORD LOAM turns up to below the tea-table and hands the cake-plate to LADY AGATHA, then moving down to the upstage end of the L. settee.)

LORD LOAM *(to TOMPSETT)*. And how are all at home?

(During the next lines LADY MARY returns below the table to the L.C. armchair and sits while LADY AGATHA goes to CRICHTON up L.C. to ask him if he will take tea. He bows. She returns to the table— business with cups.)

TOMPSETT *(during the above)*. Fairish, my lord, if 'tis the horses you are inquiring for.

LORD LOAM. No, no—the family. How's the baby?

TOMPSETT. Blooming, your lordship.

LORD LOAM. A very fine boy. *(Several of the SERVANTS hear this, look up, and suppress smiles.)* I remember saying so when I saw him—nice little chap.

TOMPSETT. Beg pardon, my lord, it's a girl.

LORD LOAM. A girl? Aha! ha! ha!—Exactly what I said. I distinctly remember saying if it's spared it will be a girl. *(He carries this off, crossing to C. The others suppress laughter. The PAGE BOY looks and grins at ELIZA. TOMPSETT and MRS. PERKINS exchange glances and smiles. LORD LOAM turns up R.C., to R. of CRICHTON.)* Very delighted to see you, Crichton. *(He offers CRICHTON his hand, who hesitates before taking it.)* Mary, do you know Mr. Crichton?

(CRICHTON *comes down to* R. *of the armchair* L.C.
LADY MARY *rises and pours him out a cup of tea.*
LORD LOAM *crosses down* R. *to* FISHER *and* FLEURY.
*The former rises on his approach and then sits
again.*)

LADY MARY. Milk and sugar, Crichton?
CRICHTON. I'm ashamed to be seen talking to you,
my lady.
LADY MARY. To such a perfect servant as you, all
this must be most distasteful. *(She hands him a cup of
tea.* CRICHTON *is too respectful to answer.)* Oh, please
to speak or I shall have to recite—you do hate it, don't
you?
CRICHTON *(taking the tea).* It pains me, your ladyship. It disturbs the etiquette of the servants' hall.
After last month's meeting, the page boy, in a burst
of equality, called me Crichton. He was dismissed.
LADY MARY *(sitting in the chair* L.C.). I wonder—
I really do—how you can remain with us.

(LADY AGATHA *is now talking to* MRS. PERKINS *over
the settee.*)

CRICHTON (R. *of* LADY MARY). I should have felt
compelled to give notice, my lady, if master had not
had a seat in the Upper House. I cling to that.

(There is a pause. LORD LOAM *looks around and coughs.*
LADY MARY *offers* CRICHTON *some cake, rising as*
LADY AGATHA *busies herself with the* STABLE
BOY *and the* KITCHEN WENCH. LADY CATHERINE
offers cake to ELIZA *and* SIMMONS *over the back
of the* R. *settee and then returns to* TREHERNE.
LORD LOAM *moves across up* C., *and then to up* L.,
beaming around. At the same time, ERNEST *is
moving from one to the other at* R., *eventually
reaching* THOMAS, *talking to him on his* R., *over
the* R. *settee.)*

LADY MARY. Do go on speaking. *(She gives* CRICHTON *more milk.)* Tell me, what did Mr. Ernest mean by saying he was too young to know everything?

CRICHTON. I have no idea, my lady.

LADY MARY. But you laughed.

CRICHTON. My lady, he is the second son of a peer.

LADY MARY. Very proper sentiments. You are a good soul, Crichton. *(She sits again.)*

(LORD LOAM has come down to the KITCHEN WENCH and GLADYS at L., and then to MRS. PERKINS, talking to her below the L. settee.)

LORD BROCKLEHURST *(desperately to* ELIZA, *with whom he has been trying to make conversation).* And now tell me—what sort of weather have you been having in the kitchen? *(The* PAGE BOY *is much amused.)* Have you been to the opera? Do you enjoy the Great Wheel? *(*ELIZA *gurgles.)* For Heaven's sake, woman, be articulate.

(There is no response to this. LORD BROCKLEHURST *rises, gives a despairing glance at* TREHERNE, *and crosses up* C., *wiping his brow, working over to* R. *near* ERNEST, *who joins him with* TREHERNE. *At the same time* LADY CATHERINE *speaks to* ELIZA *over the back of the settee, seeing she is very hot, and then crosses* L., *opens the windows, and returns to* ELIZA *with a fresh cup of tea. Meanwhile,* LORD LOAM *has left* MRS. PERKINS, *and reached the table, standing above it with* LADY AGATHA *on his left. The* STABLE BOY *has left his stool and is* L., *talking to the* KITCHEN WENCH.)*

CRICHTON *(still talking to* LADY MARY). No, my lady, his lordship may compel us to be equal upstairs— *(*LORD LOAM *is moving across up stage towards* R.) but there will never be equality in the servants' hall.

(LORD LOAM *checks up* R.C., *and comes down* R. *of*
CRICHTON, *some paces from him.*)

LORD LOAM *(coming down* C.*)*. What's that? No
equality? Can't you see, Crichton, that our divisions into
classes are artificial; that if we were to return to nature
—which is the aspiration of my life—all would be
equal.

(Some of the SERVANTS *who have been quietly con-
versing, stop, and turn to listen.)*

CRICHTON. If I may make so bold as to contradict
your lordship.
LORD LOAM *(with an effort)*. Go on.
CRICHTON. The divisions into classes, my lord, are
not artificial. They are the natural outcome of a civilized
society. There must always be a master and servants
in all civilized communities, my lord, for it is natural,
and whatever is natural is right.
LORD LOAM *(tartly)*. It is very unnatural for me to
stand here and allow you to talk such nonsense.

(ERNEST *has crossed up* R.C.)

CRICHTON *(eagerly)*. That is what I have been striv-
ing to point out to your lordship.

(LADY MARY *takes* CRICHTON'S *cup, and moves with
it below and up* L. *of the table.* CRICHTON *moves
respectfully towards* LORD LOAM, *who is ponder-
ing, finding himself in a quandary. He then crosses
below and to the* L. *of* CRICHTON, *taking out the
notes for his speech.* CRICHTON *quietly places the
hassock above and slightly on the* R. *of the armchair* L.C., *and* LORD LOAM *turns up and stands on
it. There is some restlessness among the company,
the putting down of cups, and unhappy anticipa-
tion of the coming speech.)*

LORD LOAM (*holding up his hand for silence—clears his throat—addresses the company*). My friends— (*The* KITCHEN WENCH *says,* "'ear, 'ear!" *but is checked by* CRICHTON's *look of disapproval.*) I am glad to see you all looking so happy. It used to be predicted by the scoffer, that these meetings would prove distasteful to you—are they distasteful? I hear you laughing at the question. (ALL *are silent. He looks round, in surprise.* CRICHTON *gives a short unnatural laugh and the* OTHERS *follow suit.*) No harm in saying now that among us to-day is one who was formerly hostile to the movement, but who to-day has been conquered. I am sure Lord Brocklehurst—— (ALL *turn and look at* LORD BROCKLEHURST, *the* SERVANTS *at back rising to get a sight of him.*) will presently say to me that if the charming lady now by his side has derived as much pleasure from his company as he has derived from hers he will be more than satisfied. (LORD BROCKLEHURST, *standing above* ELIZA, *shows his teeth—* ELIZA *trembles.*) For the time being the artificial and unnatural—I say unnatural— (*he glares at* CRICHTON. CRICHTON *bows slightly.*) barriers of society are swept away. Would that they could be swept away for ever. (ERNEST *moves to above the* L. *end of the* R. *settee.*)

PAGE BOY. 'Ear, 'ear!

LORD LOAM (*turns to the* PAGE BOY—*looks—speaks emphatically*). But that is entirely and utterly out of the question. And now for a few months we are to be separated. (*The* PAGE BOY *turns to* ELIZA, *rubbing his hands—the* OTHERS *also show delight.*) As you know, my daughters and Mr. Ernest and Mr. Treherne are to accompany me on my yacht on a voyage to distant parts of the earth. In less than forty-eight hours we shall be under way. (*Cheers.*) Do not think our life on the yacht is to be one long idle holiday. My views on the excessive luxury of the day are well known, and what I preach I am resolved to practice. I have therefore decided that my daughters, instead of having one maid each, as at present, shall, on this voyage, have but one maid between them.

(JEANNE rises and looks at SIMMONS and FISHER— they also look at each other.)

LADY MARY *(rises)*. Father!
LADY AGATHA. Father!
LADY CATHERINE. Father! *(She half rises).* } *(almost together)*
CRICHTON. My lord!
LORD LOAM. My mind is made up.
ERNEST. I cordially agree.

(The GIRLS look daggers at ERNEST.)

LORD LOAM. And now, my friends, I should like to think that there is something I could give each of you to take away. *(The PAGE BOY pounces on a large piece of cake.)* Not cake. *(He crosses to him.)* Some thought, some noble saying, over which you might ponder in my absence. *(He pats the PAGE BOY on the head and returns to his place. CRICHTON takes the cake from the PAGE BOY and places it on the table up L. and returns to C.)* In this connection I remember a proverb, which has had a great effect on my own life—I first heard it many years ago—I have never forgotten it, it constantly cheers and guides me. That proverb is—that proverb was—the proverb I speak of——

(LORD LOAM taps his forehead. ALL look uncomfortably at one another.)

LADY MARY *(after looking at LORD LOAM, half rises).* Oh dear—I believe he has forgotten it. *(She sits again.)*
LORD LOAM. The proverb—that proverb—the proverb to which I refer—— *(There is general distress. CRICHTON gives short applause, looking around at the SERVANTS as a sign for them to follow suit, which they*

do rather half-heartedly. LORD LOAM *becomes more and more desperate.*) I have it now. (ALL *strain forward, thinking he has remembered, but he cannot recall it.*)

LADY MARY *(rises).* Crichton!

(She indicates to him to dismiss the servants. CRICHTON *moves down a little and signs, first to* MRS. PERKINS *down* L., *and then to* SIMMONS *at* R. *All the* SERVANTS *rise. The* PAGE BOY *replaces his stool nearer the table, and stands there as* ELIZA *passes him to up* C. *Then he goes up and stares into* LORD LOAM'S *face until* CRICHTON *pushes him off. So far as possible the general exeunt is in the same order as the entrances, and is quick and silent. During all this,* LORD LOAM, *with his right arm uplifted, is making efforts to remember the proverb. As the last servant leaves,* CRICHTON *takes* LORD LOAM'S *right arm, places it on his own, and moving with him to* C., *says:*)

CRICHTON. Mr. Treherne.

*(*TREHERNE *crosses and takes* LORD LOAM'S *left arm, and they conduct his Lordship off up* R.C.*)*

LORD LOAM *(as they turn to go up* R.C.*).* The proverb ——it was—one moment, *etc.——— (Until off.)*

LADY MARY *(coming down* L.C. *below the table).* One maid among three grown women! *(She turns to below the* L. *settee.)*

*(*ERNEST *crosses up to the table* L.C., *and eats a biscuit,* LORD BROCKLEHURST *is pettish—*ERNEST *is sulky and in the position from which he was to make his speech. The three* GIRLS *have collapsed.* LADY AGATHA *on the chair above the table.* LADY CATHERINE *on the* R. *settee.)*

LORD BROCKLEHURST *(rising, crossing to* C.*)*. Mary, I think I had better go. That dreadful kitchenmaid!

LADY MARY *(crossing to him, on his* L.*)*. I can't blame you, George.

(They kiss coldly and LADY MARY *crosses below the settee to* R. LORD BROCKLEHURST *then bows to the* OTHERS *and goes up* C. *He checks there and turns to* LADY MARY.*)*

LORD BROCKLEHURST. Your father's views are shocking to me, and I am glad I am not to be one of the party on the yacht. My respect for myself, Mary—my natural anxiety as to what Mother will say—I shall see you, darling, before you sail.

(Exit LORD BROCKLEHURST L.C.*)*

ERNEST *(at* C., *looking after him, kicking the hassock to* R.*)*. Selfish brute—only thinking of himself. What about my speech?

LADY MARY *(crossing and sitting in the chair* R.C.*)*. One maid among three of us! *(Tragically.)* What's to be done!

ERNEST. Pooh! You must do for yourselves—that's all.

LADY MARY. Do for ourselves—how can we know where our things are kept?

LADY AGATHA *(rising)*. Are you aware that dresses button up the back? *(She comes down* L. *of the tea-table.)*

LADY CATHERINE. How are we to get into our boots and be prepared for the carriage?

LADY MARY. Who is to put us to bed, and who is to get us up, and how shall we ever know it's morning if there is no one to pull up the blinds?

*(*LADY CATHERINE *rises and goes down to the fireplace.* CRICHTON *re-enters up* R.C. ERNEST *and the* GIRLS *turn to him.)*

ERNEST. How is his Lordship now?

CRICHTON *(closing the door)*. A little easier, sir. *(He crosses towards the doors up* L.C.*)*.

LADY MARY *(rising)*. Crichton, send Fisher to me.

(CRICHTON bows and exits L.C., *leaving the doors open.)*

ERNEST *(coming down* C. *again)*. I have no pity for you girls, I——

LADY MARY *(turning away and throwing herself on the settee* R.C.*)*. Ernest, go away and don't insult the broken-hearted.

ERNEST. And uncommon glad I am to go. Ta, ta, all of you. *(He goes up* C., *and turns below the doors.)* He asked me to say a few words—I came here to say a few words—and I'm not at all sure that I couldn't bring an action against him.

(He exits, closes the doors after him.)

LADY MARY *(hearing the doors shut, thinks out a plan, rises, crosses and sits in the armchair* L.C.*)*. My poor sisters, come here. *(They go to her doubtfully.* LADY CATHERINE *on her right.* LADY AGATHA *stands below the table on her left. She is now quite the mother to them.)* We must make this draw us closer together. I shall do my best to help you in every way. Just now I cannot think of myself at all.

LADY AGATHA *(looks at her in surprise)*. But how unlike you, Mary!

LADY MARY *(looking up at her)*. It is my duty to protect my sisters. *(Giving her a sisterly smile.)*

LADY CATHERINE. I never knew her so sweet before, Agatha. *(She takes her hand.)* What do you propose to do, dearest Mary?

LADY MARY. I propose, when we are on the yacht, to lend Fisher to you, when I don't need her myself.

LADY AGATHA *(rising)*. Fisher?

LADY MARY. Of course, as the eldest, I have decided that it is *my* maid we shall take with us.

LADY CATHERINE *(backing a pace)*. Mary, you toad. *(She goes down* L., *below the* L. *settee.)*

LADY AGATHA *(to above the* R. *end of the* L. *settee).* Nothing on earth would induce Fisher to lift her hand for either me or Catherine.

LADY MARY *(languidly)*. Dear Agatha— *(swinging her foot)* I was afraid of it. That is why I am so sorry for you. *(Her sisters turn as if about to speak, but* FISHER'S *entrance stops them. She enters* C. *and closes the doors and crosses to* C. LADY MARY *rises, smiling triumphantly and crosses to the table* L. *of the* R. *settee for a book and paper knife.* LADY CATHERINE *sits down* L.C. LADY AGATHA *crosses to behind the settee* L., *near her. Turning to* FISHER.*)* Fisher, you heard what his Lordship said?

FISHER *(at* C.*).* Yes, my lady?

(LADY CATHERINE *and* LADY AGATHA *notice* FISHER'S
manner.)

LADY MARY *(coming and sitting on the chair* L. *of the settee* R., *with her back to* FISHER, *languidly)*. You have given me some satisfaction of late, Fisher, and to mark my approval I have decided you shall be the maid who accompanies us.

FISHER. I thank you, my lady.

LADY MARY *(sees* FISHER *still standing)*. That is all —you may go.

FISHER. If you please, my lady, I wish to give notice.

(LADY CATHERINE *and* LADY AGATHA *are delighted—*
LADY AGATHA *whispers to* LADY CATHERINE *and
then goes up to behind the table* L.C.*)*

LADY MARY *(starts—then is coldly indignant)*. Oh, certainly—you may go. *(She lifts her book and reads.)*

LADY CATHERINE. But why, Fisher?

FISHER *(turning to* LADY CATHERINE*).* I could not undertake, my lady, to wait upon three. We don't do it. *(In an indignant outburst to* LADY MARY*.)* Oh, my lady, to think that this affront—

LADY MARY *(looking up coldly).* I thought I told you to go, Fisher.

*(*FISHER *stands for a moment irresolute. Then she turns and exits* L.C., *rather huffily, leaving the doors open. As soon as she has gone,* LADY MARY *puts down her book—the* OTHERS *gloat over her.)*

LADY AGATHA *(crossing to above the settee* R.C.*).* Serves you right.

(Enter CRICHTON C., *closing the doors.)*

LADY CATHERINE *(rising).* It will be Simmons after all. *(She moves up to the armchair* L.C. LADY AGATHA *up* R., *shows annoyance and comes down* R. *of the settee.* CRICHTON *comes to* C. *To* CRICHTON.*)* Send Simmons to me.

CRICHTON *(coming down* C. *a little, after hesitating).* My lady, might I venture to speak?

LADY CATHERINE. What is it?

CRICHTON *(to* LADY CATHERINE*).* I happen to know, your ladyship, that Simmons desires to give notice for the same reason as Fisher.

LADY CATHERINE. Oh! *(She sits* L.C. *in the armchair.)*

LADY AGATHA *(below the* R. *settee, triumphant).* Then, Catherine, we take Jeanne.

CRICHTON. And Jeanne also, my lady.

(There is general gloom, but though LADY CATHERINE *and* LADY AGATHA *give way to their emotions before* CRICHTON, LADY MARY *is always cold and haughty.)*

LADY AGATHA. Oh! Oh! Oh! *(She sits, infuriated, on the* R. *settee.)* We can't blame them. Could *any* maid, who respected herself, be got to wait upon three?

LADY MARY. I suppose there are such persons, Crichton?

CRICHTON *(guardedly)*. I have heard, my lady, that there are such.

LADY MARY *(a little desperate)*. Crichton, what's to be done? We sail in two days—could one be discovered in the time?

(CRICHTON reflects.)

LADY AGATHA *(to CRICHTON)*. Surely you can think of someone.

CRICHTON *(makes a movement with his hands— heavily)*. There is in this establishment, your ladyship, a young woman——

LADY MARY *(all the GIRLS look at one another)*. Yes?

CRICHTON. A young woman on whom I have for some time cast an eye.

LADY CATHERINE *(rising; eagerly)*. Do you mean as a possible lady's maid?

CRICHTON. I had thought of her, my lady, in— *(Coughs)* another connection.

LADY MARY. Ah!

(The GIRLS exchange glances.)

CRICHTON. But I believe her to be quite the young person you require. If you could see her, my lady.

LADY MARY. I shall certainly see her. Bring her to me. *(Exit CRICHTON up* L.C.*)* You two needn't wait.

LADY CATHERINE *(crossing to* L. *of LADY MARY's chair)*. Needn't we! *(She goes down to the fireplace.)* We see your little game, Mary.

LADY AGATHA *(rising and going to the* L. *end of the settee* R.*)*. We shall certainly remain and have our two-thirds of her. Catherine, let us stick together. *(Moving down* R. *to LADY CATHERINE.)*

(They take hands and defy LADY MARY, *who rises, stamps her foot, then sits, as* CRICHTON *enters with* ELIZA *on his* L. CRICHTON *enters* C., *leaving the doors open, showing in* ELIZA, *who is quaking with self-consciousness. She regards* CRICHTON *as a god, and curtseys to him.)*

CRICHTON (L *of the chair* R.C.). This, my lady, is the young person.

LADY CATHERINE. Oh!

(All THREE *show that they consider her quite unsuitable.* LADY AGATHA *moves to the* R. *end of the settee.)*

LADY MARY. Come here, girl—— *(*ELIZA, *down* C. *below and* L. *of* CRICHTON, *does not move.)* Don't be afraid.

*(*CRICHTON *brings her forward—she keeps her eyes on him; he crosses her to* R.C. *She bobs, he breaks to* C. *His manner is that of one who knows himself to be her superior but who, nevertheless, has a genuine pride in her.)*

CRICHTON *(turning at* L.C.). Her appearance, my lady, is homely, and her manners, as you may have observed, deplorable, but she has a heart of gold.

(This is said openly before ELIZA *and in the tone of one honestly doing his best for her—she is gratified.)*

LADY MARY. What is your position downstairs?

*(*ELIZA *turns to* LADY MARY *and mutters nervously, then turns an appealing face to* CRICHTON.)*

CRICHTON *(kindly).* Speak up, speak up.

ELIZA (*bobs*). Yes, sir. (*She turns to* LADY MARY.) I'm a tweeny, your ladyship.

LADY CATHERINE. A what?

ELIZA. Er—er—— (*She looks at* CRICHTON *again appealingly and fingers her dress nervously.*) A tweeny!

CRICHTON (*takes a step forward*). A tweeny, that is to say, my lady, she is not at present, strictly speaking, anything—a between-maid, she helps the vegetable maid. It is she, my lady, who transfers the dishes from the one end of the kitchen table where they are placed by the cook, to the other end where they enter into the charge of Thomas and John.

LADY MARY. I see. And you and Crichton are—ah—keeping company.

(CRICHTON *draws himself up, hurt.*)

ELIZA (*aghast*). A butler don't keep company, my lady.

LADY MARY (*impatiently*). Does he not?

CRICHTON. No, your ladyship, we butlers may— (*he makes a gesture with his arms*) but we do not keep company.

LADY CATHERINE (*sits on the arm of the chair below the fireplace*). I know what it is—you are engaged?

(ELIZA *looks longingly at* CRICHTON.)

CRICHTON. Certainly not, my lady. The utmost I can say at present is that I have cast a favorable eye.

(ELIZA *is in ecstasies.*)

LADY MARY (*indifferently*). As you choose. But I'm afraid, Crichton, *she* will not suit *us*.

(ELIZA *shows her disappointment.*)

CRICHTON (*a little hotly*). My lady, beneath this simple exterior are concealed a very sweet nature and rare womanly gifts.

LADY AGATHA. Unfortunately that is not what we want.

CRICHTON. And it is she, my lady, who dresses the hair of the ladies' maids for our evening meals.

(ALL *show interest.* LADY CATHERINE *rises, taking a pace towards* LADY AGATHA, *who turns to her.*)

LADY MARY *(quickly)*. She dresses Fisher's hair?

ELIZA. Yes, my lady, and I does them up when they goes to parties.

CRICHTON *(pained at her language)*. Does!

ELIZA. Doos. *(To* LADY MARY.*)* And it's me what alters your gowns to fit 'em.

CRICHTON *(again pained)*. *What* alters?

ELIZA. *(greatly distressed)*. Which alters.

LADY AGATHA. Mary!

LADY MARY. I shall certainly have her.

LADY CATHERINE. *We* shall certainly have you. Tweeny, we have decided to make a lady's maid of you.

ELIZA *(delighted)*. Oh, lawks!

LADY AGATHA. We are doing this for you so that your position socially may be more nearly akin to that of Crichton.

ELIZA. Oh!

CRICHTON *(gravely)*. It will undoubtedly increase the young person's chances.

LADY MARY. Then if I get a good character for you from Mrs. Perkins, she will make all arrangements. *(She resumes her reading.)*

ELIZA *(glorious)*. My lady!

LADY MARY. By the way, I hope you are a good sailor.

ELIZA *(startled)*. You don't mean, my lady—I'm to go on the ship?

LADY MARY. Certainly.

ELIZA. But—— *(To* CRICHTON.*)* You ain't going, sir?

CRICHTON. No.

ELIZA *(alarmed)* Then neither ain't I.

LADY AGATHA *(crosses to* L. *of the chair* R.C.*).* You must!

ELIZA *(moves to* CRICHTON*).* Leave him! Not me!

(LADY AGATHA turns up, to above the L. *end of the settee.)*

LADY MARY. Girl, don't be silly. Crichton will be—considered in your wages.

ELIZA. I ain't going.

CRICHTON. I feared this, my lady.

ELIZA. Nothink'll budge me.

LADY MARY *(angrily).* Leave the room. (CRICHTON *crosses to* LADY MARY.) Put her out!

(The sharpness of the order displeases CRICHTON, *and he shows* ELIZA *out with marked politeness, indicating the doors up* L.C., *and conducting her to them. She exits. He closes the doors and then returns to* C. *The* SISTERS *are gloomy.)*

LADY AGATHA *(moving* C. *to* R. *of* CRICHTON*).* Crichton—— (CRICHTON *checks.*) I think you might have shown more displeasure.

CRICHTON *(contrite).* I was touched, your ladyship. I see, my lady, that to part from her would be a wrench to me, though I could not well say so in her presence, not yet having decided how far I shall go with her.

(LADY AGATHA crosses to below the table L.C. CRICHTON *is about to turn up* L.C., *when* LORD LOAM *enters in a passion up* R.C.*)*

LORD LOAM *(coming down* C.*).* The ingrate! The smug! The fop!

LADY CATHERINE *(down* R.C.*).* What is it now, Father?

LORD LOAM. That man of mine, Rolleston, refuses

to accompany us because you are to have but one maid.

LADY AGATHA. Hurrah! (*She moves round to* L *of the tea-table.*)

(LORD LOAM *glares at her. The* GIRLS *look delightedly at one another.*)

LADY MARY (*rising and crossing his arm*). Darling Father, rather than you should lose Rolleston, we will consent to take all three of them.

LORD LOAM (*pushing her off*). Pooh—nonsense. (LADY MARY *moves away to up* R.C. *Crossing to below the armchair* L.C.) Crichton! (CRICHTON *comes down* C.) Find me a valet who can do without three maids. (*He sits in the armchair.*)

CRICHTON. Yes, my lord. (*Troubled.*) In the time— the more suitable— (LADY AGATHA *beckons* LADY MARY *to come round the back of above the table* L.C.) the party, my lord, the less willing will he be to come without the usual perquisites.

LORD LOAM. Anyone will do. (*He rises and goes to the windows down* L.)

CRICHTON (*shocked*). My lord!

(LADY MARY *hurries across to* LADY AGATHA *up* L.C.)

LORD LOAM (*in an exasperated tone, looking out of the window*). The ingrate! The puppy!

LADY AGATHA (*with sudden idea*). Mary! (*She whispers to her across the table.*)

LADY MARY. I ask a favor of a servant—never. (*She crosses back to the settee.*)

LADY AGATHA (*crossing* C., *as* CRICHTON *moves below the chair*). Crichton, would it not be very distressing to you to let his Lordship go, attended by a valet who might prove unworthy? (CRICHTON *turns* R., *to face her.*) It is only for three months—don't you think that you—you—— (*As* CRICHTON *sees what she wants he pulls himself up with noble offended dignity, and she is appalled.)* I beg your pardon.

(CRICHTON *bows stiffly and backs a step or two.* LORD
LOAM *paces fretfully up* L.)

LADY CATHERINE *(to* CRICHTON, *moving in a pace).*
But think of the joy of Tweeny.

(CRICHTON *is moved, but shakes his head.* LADY CATH-
ERINE *turns away down* R.)

LADY MARY *(above the* R. *settee).* Crichton! *(She
leans over and gets her books—moves* R., *and sits on the
settee.)* Do you think it safe to let the master you love
go so far away without you, while he has these dangerous views about equality?

(CRICHTON *hesitates, profoundly stirred.* LADY AGATHA
and LADY CATHERINE *almost beg him with their
hands—*LADY MARY *is also really eager, but when
he looks at her, she coldly opens the book and
begins to read.* CRICHTON *turns up* C. *a few paces,
obviously having an inward struggle. He checks,
and turns down to* LORD LOAM, *who is now chafing
at* L. *of the table* L.C. LADY AGATHA *quietly slips
across to above the chair* L. *of the* R. *settee and
watches.)*

CRICHTON. My lord! (LORD LOAM *turns, and crosses
to below the settee.)* I have found a man.

LORD LOAM *(crossing to below the chair* L.C.). Already? Who is he? (CRICHTON *presents himself with a
gesture.)* Yourself?

LADY CATHERINE *(coming to a pace).* Father, how
good of him.

LORD LOAM *(pleased, but thinking it a small thing).*
Uncommon good. Thank you, Crichton! *(He crosses
up* C., R. *of* CRICHTON, *who bows.* LADY AGATHA *moves*

above the settee to LADY MARY. *Turning up* C., *to*
CRICHTON.) This helps me nicely out of a hole, and
it will annoy Rolleston. Come with me and we shall
tell him. (*He turns towards the door up* R.C.) Not that
I think you have lowered yourself in any way. Come
along.

(*Exit* LORD LOAM R.C. CRICHTON *is about to follow,
    when* LADY AGATHA *crosses to* C. *and speaks to
    him.*)

LADY AGATHA. Crichton! (*She holds out her hand.*)
Thank you.
CRICHTON. My lady—a valet's hand.

(LADY MARY *turns her head to look. He won't shake
    hands—he is suffering from deep genuine emotion.*
    LADY AGATHA *and* LADY CATHERINE *are a little
    touched.* LADY MARY *is rather curious.*)

LADY AGATHA (*after a look at* LADY CATHERINE
and LADY MARY). I had no idea you would feel it so
deeply—why did you do it?

(CRICHTON *is too respectful to reply.*)

LADY MARY (*rising*). Crichton! (CRICHTON *comes
down a little* L. *of* C. *Taking a pace to* R.C.) I am curious,
I *insist* upon an answer.

(LADY AGATHA *moves to above the chair* R.C. LADY
    CATHERINE *comes in a pace towards* LADY MARY,
    below and on her R.)

CRICHTON. My lady, I am the son of a butler and a
lady's maid—perhaps the happiest of all combinations—
(*The* GIRLS *laugh to themselves.*) and to me the most
beautiful thing in the world is a haughty aristocratic
English house with everyone kept in his place. Though
I were equal to your ladyship—where would be the

pleasure to me?—it would be more than counterbalanced by the pain of feeling that Thomas and John were equal to *me*.

LADY CATHERINE. But Father says if we were to return to nature——

CRICHTON. If we did, my lady, the first thing we should do would be to elect a head. Circumstances might alter cases—the same person might not be master —the same person might not be servants. I cannot say as to that, nor indeed should we have the deciding of it. Nature would decide it for us.

LADY MARY. You seem to have thought it all out carefully, Crichton. *(She moves a cushion to the L. end of the settee and puts her feet up on the R. end.)*

CRICHTON. Yes, my lady. *(He backs a step.)*

LADY CATHERINE. And you have done this for us, Crichton, because you thought that—that Father needed to be kept in his place?

CRICHTON. I should prefer you to say, my lady, that I have done it—for the house.

LADY AGATHA. Thank you, Crichton. *(She crosses above and to R. of LADY MARY at the back of the settee.)* Mary— *(She wants LADY MARY to be kind but LADY MARY has begun to read again. LADY AGATHA returns to L. of the chair R.C. CRICHTON moves up C. To CRICHTON.)* If there was any way in which we could show our gratitude.   *(WARN Curtain.)*

CRICHTON *(moves down a little)*. If I might venture, my lady, would you kindly show it by becoming more like Lady Mary. *(Looking at her.)* That disdain is what we like from our superiors. Even so do we, the upper servants, disdain the lower servants, while they take it out of the odds and ends.

(Exit CRICHTON up L.C. The GIRLS become lazy again.)

LADY AGATHA *(crossing down L.)*. Oh dear, what a tiring day! *(She sits on the lower end of the settee, putting her feet up.)*

LADY CATHERINE (*crossing* L. *to the same settee*). I feel dead. Tuck in your feet, you selfish thing. (*She sits at the upper end, putting her feet up on the downstage end, to* LADY AGATHA'S *discomfort.*)

(LADY MARY *is lying reading on the other settee. They are* ALL *sleepy. A pause.*)

LADY MARY (*looking up from her book*). I wonder what he meant by circumstances might alter cases?

LADY AGATHA (*yawns*). But don't talk, Mary—I was nearly asleep.

(*A pause.*)

LADY MARY (*sleepily*). I wonder what he meant by the same person might not be master and the same persons might not be servants?

LADY CATHERINE. Do be quiet, Mary, and leave it to Nature—he said Nature would decide.

(*A pause—she turns and snuggles into the pillows.*)

LADY MARY (*sleepily*). I wonder——— (*She tries to read, but her eyes close and the book drops on to her lap, and then it and the paper knife roll on to the floor.*)

LADY AGATHA (*almost asleep*). What?

All seem to be asleep, as—

The CURTAIN *falls.*

ACT II

Scene.—*The Island.*

Two months have elapsed and the scene is a tropical island on which the travellers have been wrecked. The actual place is a wild spot in a wood which stretches far away on both sides, the trees being bread-fruit, banana, coco-nut, etc. The ground is a dense tangle of long grass growing about six feet high, bamboo and prickly coarse vegetation, and at the rise of the Curtain *this seems to cover the stage and shuts out most of the view at back. Thus, at the opening, the sea is not seen though it is really on the back cloth. In the stillness of the opening, however, the splash of the waves can be heard, adding melancholy to the scene. The whole effect should be one of desolation and discomfort. The wood around is mysterious, sullen, dangerous.*

As far as possible the scene should convey the impression that horrible animals prowl in the woods and that snakes may come out of the grass. In the background on R. *a rude hut is in course of erection, but at present only the top of it is seen owing to the denseness of the vegetation in front.*

At L.C., *low rocks rise to higher ledges leading off* L., *through the trees and jungle vegetation. At* C., *there is a bucket, with a board across it to form a seat. Slightly below it, at* R.C., *a large tripod of stout branches indicates where a fire has been made. An iron pot hangs from the tripod. The grass in the centre acting area has been cut down somewhat, but elsewhere, up stage and on either side, it is very long indeed.*

When the CURTAIN *rises,* TREHERNE *can be seen now and again on the roof of the hut, building it with logs and rough planks for which he descends from time to time.*

LADY MARY, LADY AGATHA *and* LADY CATHERINE *are seated on the lower rocks at* L.C. LADY MARY *is between the others with* LADY CATHERINE *slightly below and on her* L., *and* LADY AGATHA *perched a little higher and on her* R. ERNEST *is seated on the bucket, writing on a piece of paper.* ALL *are dressed eccentrically in such confused garments as people roused from sleep by shipwreck might fling on or have flung on them. Thus, one lady has a common sailor's blue jacket over a skirt. Another wears a jersey and a sailor's red cap. The third wears a long ulster to cover half a dress underneath. They wear bath slippers, etc.—all hopelessly bad for a prickly jungle. They walk as if on needles. The* MEN *dress to correspond and are unshaven. No one has boots.*

The sun is streaming down, and TREHERNE *seems very hot, but the* OTHERS, *not working, are cool. During the opening scene,* TREHERNE *is joined occasionally by* CRICHTON *about the hut structure. This hut, it should be noted, has the makings of a window opening facing down stage, and a rough door opening in the wall facing* L. *As the scene commences, the sea is heard, and the knocking of hammers on wood about the hut.*

ERNEST *(looking up from his writing and across at the ladies).* This is what I have written—listen! *(*TREHERNE *disappears.)* "Wrecked, wrecked, wrecked! On an island in the tropics— *(the sound of the sea dies away)* the Hon. Ernest Woolley, the Rev. John Treherne, the Ladies Mary, Catherine and Agatha Lasenby, with two servants. Sole survivors of Lord Loam's steam yacht 'Bluebell'— *(*LADY CATHERINE *and* LADY AGATHA *sob;* LADY MARY *comforts them.)*—which encountered a fearful gale in these seas and soon became a total wreck. The crew behaved gallantly, putting us all into the first boat. What became of them I cannot tell, but we, after dreadful sufferings, and insufficiently clad in whatever garments we could lay hold of in the dark——"

LADY MARY *(drawing her clothes about her)*. Please don't describe our garments.

ERNEST. "——succeeded in reaching this island with the loss of one of our party. *(The* LADIES *look at one another and then sob.)* Namely, Lord Loam. *(The* LADIES *weep louder.* LADY CATHERINE *leans her head on* LADY MARY'S *shoulder and* LADY AGATHA *hers on* LADY MARY'S *knee.)* Who flung away his life in a gallant attempt to save a servant who had fallen overboard."

(The GIRLS *dry their eyes and look up.)*

LADY AGATHA *(strongly)*. But, Ernest, it was Crichton who jumped into the sea trying to save *Father*.

ERNEST. Well, you know it was rather silly of Uncle to fling away his life trying to get into the boat first; *(*LADY AGATHA *puts her head down.)* and as this document may be printed in the papers, it struck me—an English peer, you know.

LADY MARY. Ernest, that's very thoughtful of you.

ERNEST. "By night the cries of wild cats, the hissing of snakes, terrify us extremely— *(He scratches out writing)* terrify the *ladies* extremely. Against these we have no weapons except one cutlass and a hatchet. A bucket washed ashore is at present our only comfortable seat——"

LADY MARY. And Ernest is sitting on it.

ERNEST. Sh! Oh, do be quiet. It's utterly impossible for me to go on with all these rotten interruptions. It's sickening—that's the word—sickening! "To add to our horrors, night falls suddenly in these parts, and it is then that savage animals begin to prowl and roar."

LADY MARY *(comforting the other two* GIRLS*)*. Have you said that vampire bats suck the blood from our toes as we sleep?

*(*TREHERNE *mounts the hut again and works at it.)*

ERNEST. Hush, that's all. *(The sea again is heard.)* I end up: "Rescue us, or we perish—rich reward. Signed, Ernest Woolley, in command of our little party. This is written on a leaf taken out of a book of poems that Crichton found in his pocket."—Fancy Crichton being a reader of poetry. Now I shall put it into the bottle and fling it into the sea. *(He puts it into the soda-water bottle, knocks in the cork and crosses with it to* R.*)* The tide is going out—mustn't miss the post. *(He calls.)* Crichton! Crichton!

*(*ERNEST *turns a little to* C. LADY AGATHA *rises and gets on to the rock above* LADY MARY. CRICHTON *enters* R. *hastily through the grass, thinking it some important matter.)*

CRICHTON. (R.C., *looking at the ladies anxiously).* Anything wrong, sir?
ERNEST. The tide, Crichton, is a postman who calls at our island twice a day for letters. Ha, ah!
CRICHTON *(after a pause).* Thank you, sir.

(He retires through the grass out of sight R. *up stage.)*

ERNEST *(crossing to the rocks* L. *and mounting them).* Poor Crichton! I sometimes think he is losing his sense of humor. *(He pulls* LADY AGATHA *up.)* Come along, Agatha.

(They exit along the rocks up L. TREHERNE *disappears behind the hut* R.*)*

LADY CATHERINE. How horribly still it is.

LADY MARY. It is best when it is still.

LADY CATHERINE *(in a fearful voice)*. Mary, I have heard that they are always still just before they *jump!*

LADY MARY. *Don't. (Distant chopping is heard— eight loud chops.* LADY MARY *and* LADY CATHERINE *rise fearfully and more* C. LADY CATHERINE *goes* R., *screams and runs back to* LADY MARY.) Ah! It is only Crichton knocking down trees.

LADY CATHERINE *(taking her hand and pulling her to* R.). Mary, let us go and *stand beside him.*

LADY MARY. Let a servant see that I am afraid!

LADY CATHERINE *(going)*. Don't then, but remember this, dear—— They often drop on one from above. Mr. Treherne! Mr. Treherne!

(Exit LADY CATHERINE *up* R.C. *and off* R. *in the direction of the knocking.* LADY MARY *looks round, moves* L., *creaking sound makes her start and run quickly to* R.)

LADY MARY. Crichton! Crichton!

(CRICHTON *forces his way through the* R. *undergrowth at the back, carrying a cutlass.)*

CRICHTON. Did you call, my lady?

(TREHERNE *is seen cutting grass at the back* R.)

LADY MARY *(concealing her agitation)*. I? *(She crosses to* L.C.) Why should I? Why should I call?

CRICHTON. My mistake, your ladyship. If you are afraid of being alone, my lady——

LADY MARY *(turning)*. Afraid? Certainly not. You may go. *(She moves to* R.C. *and sits.)*

CRICHTON. I must clear away this grass, at any rate.

(TREHERNE *cuts grass away at the back from* C. *to* L. CRICHTON *crosses up* L.C. *and starts cutting down*

grass. LADY MARY *takes off oilskin coat and sou'-
wester and fans herself, looking at* CRICHTON.
When he has made three cuts she speaks.)

LADY MARY. I wish, Crichton, you could work without looking so hot.

CRICHTON *(who is perspiring).* I wish I could, my
lady. *(Putting the grass out in heap down* L.C.*)*

LADY MARY. It makes me hot to look at you.

CRICHTON. Strange, for it almost makes me cool to
look at your ladyship. *(He goes up, cutting more grass.)*

LADY MARY. Anything I can do for you in that way,
Crichton, I shall do with pleasure.

*(*TREHERNE *moves out of sight, up* L.*)*

CRICHTON. Thank you, my lady. (LADY MARY *looks
round at the loneliness, leans on the bucket and sobs.*
CRICHTON *stops working, and comes to her down* C.*)*
Don't give way. Things might be worse, my lady.

(The sound of the sea dies away.)

LADY MARY *(in real anguish).* My poor father!

CRICHTON. If I could have given my life for his——

LADY MARY. You did all a man could do. Indeed, I
thank you, Crichton. *(With some real admiration.)*
You *are* a man.

CRICHTON. Thank you, my lady. *(He starts working
again up* C.*)*

LADY MARY *(in anguish).* But it is all so awful,
Crichton. Is there any hope of a ship coming?

CRICHTON *(stops work—after hesitation—brightly).*
Of course there is, my lady. *(He resumes work.)*

*(*LADY MARY *sees that he is saying this simply to comfort her.)*

LADY MARY *(rises).* Don't treat me as a child. *(She*

crosses up L.C.) I've got to know the worst and face it. Crichton, the truth.

CRICHTON *(dropping a pace or two down* R.C.). We were driven far out of our course, your ladyship. I fear some distance from the track of commerce.

LADY MARY *(turns away)*. Thank you. I understand. *(She is courageous but has a great struggle to control herself; she gives way to tears then pulls herself together.)*

CRICHTON *(who has been watching her, moving to* C.). You *are* a good plucked 'un, my lady!

LADY MARY *(moving down* L.). I shall try to be—— *(She stops and turns to him.)* Crichton, how dare you!

CRICHTON. I beg your ladyship's pardon, but you are! *(Laughingly.)* And until a ship does come up we three men are going to do our best for you ladies. *(He goes up and cuts the grass* R.C.)

LADY MARY. Three men? Mr. Ernest does not work.

CRICHTON *(cheerily)*. He will, my lady.

LADY MARY. I doubt it.

CRICHTON. No work—no dinner will make a great change in Mr. Ernest.

LADY MARY *(going up a little* C.). No work—no dinner! When did you invent that rule, Crichton?

CRICHTON *(still cheery)*. I didn't invent it, my lady. I seem to see it growing on the island.

LADY MARY. Crichton, your manner strikes me as curious.

(CRICHTON *stops work.*)

CRICHTON *(distressed)*. I hope not, your ladyship.

LADY MARY. You are not implying anything so unnatural I presume, as that if I and my sisters don't work there will be no dinner for *us*.

(CRICHTON *throws down the cutlass* R., *takes another bundle of grass and throws it off* R., *picks up the cutlass and goes up* L., *cutting the remaining grass.)*

CRICHTON (*during the above, after a tiny pause*). If it is unnatural, my lady, that is the end of it.

LADY MARY. If! (*Crossing to R.C. and turning to face up L.*) Now I understand! The perfect servant at home holds that we are all equal now. I see!

CRICHTON (*up L.C.; hurt*). My lady! can you think me so inconsistent?

LADY MARY. That *is* it.

CRICHTON (*taking a pace down C.*). My lady, I disbelieved in equality at home because it was against nature, and for that same reason I as utterly disbelieve in it on an island. (*He goes on cutting grass, moving up R.*)

LADY MARY. Thank you, Crichton. I apologize. (*She moves to the low rocks L.C.*)

CRICHTON (*working a little down R.C.*). There must always, my lady, be one to command and others to obey. (*He resumes work.*)

LADY MARY (*satisfied*). One to command—others to obey. (*She turns suddenly and goes quickly to CRICHTON, looking into his face.*) Crichton!

CRICHTON (*looking up*). What is it, my lady?

(LADY MARY *backs, still watching, off up L.C. behind the rocks.* CRICHTON *drops the cutlass, looks after* LADY MARY, *then goes up R. for sticks, crosses down to R. of the fire and puts some more on.* ELIZA, *now generally known as* TWEENY, *comes on singing from up L. behind the rocks and runs down to L. of the tripod.*)

TWEENY (*showing coco-nuts in her skirt*). Look what I found!

CRICHTON. Coco-nuts! Bravo!

TWEENY. They grow on trees!

CRICHTON. Where did you think they grew?

TWEENY (*making a gesture*). I thought as how they grew in rows on top of little sticks.

CRICHTON (*pained*). Oh, Tweeny, Tweeny!

TWEENY (*anxiously*). Have I offended of your feelings again, sir?

CRICHTON. A little. (*He rises and crosses up* R.C. *for sticks and comes down to the fire again—kneeling there.*)

TWEENY (*in an outburst, throws down the coconuts*). I'm full o' vulgar words and ways, and though I may keep them in their holes when you are by, as soon as I'm by myself out they come in a rush like beetles when the house is dark. (*Gestures of distress from* CRICHTON. *Crossing to the rocks* L.C., *putting one foot on them and breaking small twigs which she has picked up.*) I says them gloating like, in my head—"Blooming," I says, and "All my eye!" and "Ginger" and "Nothink" and "Shut yer mug!" and all the time we was being wrecked I was praying to myself:—"Please the Lord it may be an island as it's natural to be vulgar on!"

CRICHTON. Oh!

(*He flings up his hands—*TWEENY *becomes pathetic.*)

TWEENY. That's the kind I am, sir. (*Sitting.*) You'd better give me up.

CRICHTON (*rising and crossing to above her*). I won't give you up. It is strange indeed that one so common should attract one so fastidious, but so it is. There is something about you, Tweeny. (*A pause.*) There is a "je ne sais quoi" about you.

TWEENY (*joyous—rising on her knees and facing him*). Is there—is there?—I am glad!

CRICHTON (*putting his hands on her shoulders*). We shall fight your vulgarity together.

TWEENY. Oh, sir? (*She rises, singing, picks up coconuts and puts them* L.)

CRICHTON (*crossing to above the fire.*) Bring me some grass, Tweeny, some very dry grass.

(TWEENY *gets grass and holds it while he takes out a lens and focusses the sun's rays on to it.*)

TWEENY. What are you going to do?
CRICHTON. Light a fire.
TWEENY. What a funny way to light a fire.
CRICHTON. It may be funny, Tweeny, but it lights it all the same. Now get your head out of the way, I don't want to light that.

(When the grass lights, they BOTH *blow, and* TWEENY *puts it under the fire.)*

ERNEST *(heard outside)*. Come along, Agatha, it's all right, don't be afraid. (TWEENY *rises, goes up* C *and looks off.* ERNEST *rushes on* L. *below the rocks, followed by* LADY AGATHA—*both excited.)* Danger! Crichton, a tiger-cat!

(He crosses to R.C., *followed by* LADY AGATHA *on his* L.)*

TWEENY. Aha! *(She moves down* C. *a little.)*
CRICHTON *(who is standing down* R.C.). Where? *(He gets the cutlass.)* My God! The ladies! *(He crosses to the rocks* L.C.)
LADY AGATHA *(up* R.C.). It is at our heels.
ERNEST *(down* R.). Look out, Crichton!
CRICHTON. Quiet! (LADY MARY *and* LADY CATHERINE *enter up* L. *above the rocks, followed by* TREHERNE. *They group up* C. *and* R.C. *Speaking over his shoulder.)* Mr. Ernest says he was chased by a tiger-cat.

*(*LADY MARY *and* LADY CATHERINE *run into the hut up* R. LADY AGATHA *and* TWEENY *retreat to the lower end of the hut.* ERNEST *comes in to* R.C. *with a big stick and* TREHERNE, *who has gone up* R.C. *for a hatchet, comes to* C. CRICHTON *waits at the edge of the rock* L.C. ALL *are watching towards down* L.)*

ERNEST. It will be on us in a moment! Whish! *(Business with the stick.)*

(Heavy breathing is heard off down L.)

TREHERNE *(who has suddenly seen the grass down L. moving).* The grass is moving—listen!

(The breathing is louder. The GIRLS suppress little cries. ALL are tense. LORD LOAM crawls through the long grass down L., rises, and staggers, assisted by CRICHTON, to the bucket, where he sits exhausted.)

LORD LOAM. Oh—thank Heaven!

(The OTHERS re-group. The GIRLS run down to LORD LOAM with cries of relief and sympathy. LADY CATHERINE comes down on his R. LADY AGATHA runs across, kisses him and settles on his L. LADY MARY comes down by LADY CATHERINE and kneels above and slightly on his R. TREHERNE and ERNEST come in to R.C. while CRICHTON stands above and slightly L. of the group. TWEENY has come in a little down R. During this, the following lines are almost simultaneous:)

LADY MARY. Father?
LORD LOAM. Mary—Agatha! Oh dear, my dears! My dears—oh, dear!
LADY MARY. Darling!
LADY AGATHA. Dear Father!
LADY CATHERINE. Thank Heaven!

(As ERNEST and TREHERNE come forward and shake hands, the GIRLS fuss round LORD LOAM.)

TREHERNE. Glad to see you, sir. *(He shakes hands and moves up C., L. of the group.)*

ERNEST *(shaking hands very profusely)*. Uncle—
Uncle! Dear old Uncle—

TREHERNE *(tactlessly)*. Ernest thought you were a
tiger-cat.

LORD LOAM *(dropping his hand quickly)*. Oh, did
you! I knew you at once. I knew you by the way you
ran.

CRICHTON *(coming down* L.C., *and touching his
cap)*. My lord, I am glad, glad!

ERNEST *(down* R.*)*. But you are also idling, Crichton.
(He sits on the ground down R.*)* We mustn't waste
time—to work, to work.

CRICHTON *(after looking at him)*. Yes, sir. *(He
crosses up to the hut and disappears.)*

TREHERNE. Ernest, you be a little more civil.
Crichton, let me help.

(He crosses R., *above the group to the hut and exits up*
R., *after* CRICHTON.*)*

TWEENY *(who has come down* R.C.*)*. Oh, sir! Oh,
sir!

(She bobs to LORD LOAM *and crosses off* R., *through
the hut.)*

LORD LOAM *(seeing the pot)*. Is that—but I suppose
I'm dreaming again. *(Timidly.)* It isn't by any chance
a pot on top of a fire, is it?

LADY MARY. Indeed it is, dearest. It is our supper.

LORD LOAM *(rising)*. I have been dreaming of a pot
on top of a fire for two days. *(He goes to it, touches
it.)* —It's real! *(Timidly, turning to* LADY MARY.*)*
There's nothing in it, is there?

ERNEST. Sniff, Uncle.

LORD LOAM *(awestruck, after sniffing)*. It smells of
onions! You don't mean to say there's an onion grove
on this island?

LADY MARY. They came from the yacht.

LORD LOAM. From the yacht? Did Crichton——?

LADY CATHERINE. He swam back to her twice before she went to pieces.

LADY AGATHA. And the last time he was nearly drowned.

ERNEST (*rising*). And for what? (*He moves across up* L.C. *and turns.*) Onions! Pooh, onions are all very well in their way, but he wasted a lot of time bringing away a lot of useless truck. (*Coming down a little at* L. C.) Electric batteries, wires and all that rubbish he loaded up a raft with them, and not a single bottle of Pommery or a tin of sardines, to say nothing of some very expensive neckties hanging in full view in my stateroom!

LADY CATHERINE (*coming down to* C. *and attracting the* OTHERS' *attention*). Father—you have boots!

LADY MARY. So he has.

LORD LOAM. Of course I have.

(*He sits on the bucket again*, LADY CATHERINE *on his* L., *and* LADY AGATHA *on his* R., *sit on the grass watching the boots.* LADY MARY *stands behind.*)

ERNEST (*signing to her to be quiet*). You are actually wearing boots, Uncle. It's very unsafe, you know, in this climate.

LORD LOAM. Eh! What!

ERNEST. We have all abandoned them, you observe. The blood—the arteries, you know.

(LORD LOAM *lifts his foot*—ERNEST *kneels below and on his left, and tries to take them off.*)

LORD LOAM. I hadn't a notion.

ERNEST (*easing the left boot*). Oh Lord, yes!

LADY MARY. Father, he is trying to get your boots from you.

LORD LOAM (*pulling both feet away*). Ernest!

LADY MARY. There is nothing in the world we wouldn't give for boots.

ERNEST *(rising)*. I only wanted the loan of them.

LADY AGATHA *(cuddling on to* LORD LOAM'S R., *kneeling near* LORD LOAM). If you lend them to anyone, it will be to us, won't it, Father?

LORD LOAM *(puts his arms around her)*. Certainly, my child.

ERNEST. Oh, very well. *(Turning up* C.) I don't want your boots. *(Turning down again.)* You don't think you could spare me *one* boot, Uncle?

LORD LOAM. I do not.

ERNEST. Quite so. Well, all I can say is I'm sorry for you. *(He crosses up and lies on the rocks* L.C.)

(LADY MARY *crosses down* R.C. *and sits in front of* LORD LOAM.)

LADY MARY. Father, we thought we should never see you again.

LORD LOAM. I was washed ashore, my dear, clinging to a hencoop. How awful that first night was!

LADY MARY. Poor Father!

LORD LOAM. When I awoke, I wept. Then I began to feel—extremely hungry. There was a large turtle on the beach. I remembered from the "Swiss Family Robinson" that if you turn a turtle over, he is helpless. My dears, I crawled towards him, I flung myself upon him—— *(He pauses and rubs his leg.)* The nasty spiteful brute!

LADY MARY. You didn't turn him over?

LORD LOAM *(vindictively)*. Mary, the senseless thing wouldn't wait—I found that none of them would wait.

LADY CATHERINE. We should have been as badly off if Crichton hadn't——

LADY MARY *(quickly)*. Don't praise Crichton!

LORD LOAM. And then those beastly monkeys! I always understood that if you flung stones at them they would retaliate by flinging coco-nuts at you. Would you believe it, I flung a hundred stones and not one monkey had sufficient intelligence to grasp my meaning. How I longed for Crichton!

LADY MARY. For us also, Father?

LORD LOAM. For you also. I tried for hours to make a fire. The authors say that when wrecked on an island you can obtain a light by rubbing two pieces of stick together! *(Fiercely.)* The liars!

LADY MARY. And all the time you thought there was no one on the island but yourself.

LORD LOAM. I thought so until this morning. *(The GIRLS are interested.)* I was searching the pools for little fishes, which I caught in my hat, *(dramatically)* when I suddenly saw before me—on the sand—

LADY CATHERINE. What?

LORD LOAM. A hairpin.

(The GIRLS' hands go to their heads instinctively.)

LADY MARY. A hairpin! It must be one of ours. Give it to me, Father.

LADY AGATHA. No, it's mine!

LORD LOAM. I didn't keep it.

(Disappointed, they draw away from him, kneeling up.)

LADY MARY. Didn't keep it—found a hairpin on an island and didn't keep it.

(They draw away from him, a little farther.)

LORD LOAM. My dears?

(They move away still more. By this time TREHERNE is again visible, about the hut.)

LADY AGATHA. Oh, Father, we have returned to nature more than you bargained for.

(ERNEST *rises and strolls up* c., *looking towards the hut, pensively.*)

LADY MARY *(rising slowly)*. For shame, Agatha. *(She moves to* L. *of* LORD LOAM *and puts her arms around him.)* Don't mind her, Father. *(Anxiously looks at the hut.)* Dear, there is something I want you to do at once. (LORD LOAM *looks up.*) I mean—to assert your position as chief person on the island.

(LADY CATHERINE *rises.*)

LORD LOAM. But who would presume to question it?

LADY CATHERINE *(crossing down* R.*)*. She means Ernest. *(She turns, standing* R. *of, and below, the fire.)*

LADY MARY *(puzzled and not addressing anyone)*. Do I? *(She looks at the hut again.)*

LADY AGATHA *(to* LADY CATHERINE*)*. It's cruel to say anything against Ernest.

LORD LOAM. If anyone presumes to challenge my position I shall make short work of him.

(ERNEST, *who has not heard all this, strolls back to down* L.C.)

LADY AGATHA *(rises)*. Here comes Ernest—now see if you can say these horrid things to his face.

LORD LOAM *(confidentally)*. I shall teach him his place at once.

LADY MARY *(anxiously)*. But how?

LORD LOAM *(chuckling)*. I have just thought of an extremely amusing way of doing it. (LADY MARY *crosses to* R. *behind* LORD LOAM *and joins* LADY CATHERINE, *watching* ERNEST.) Ernest——

ERNEST *(loftily, down* L.C.*)*. Excuse me, Uncle, I'm thinking—I'm planning out the building of this hut.

LORD LOAM. I also have been thinking, Ernest.

ERNEST. That don't matter. *(With a gesture to indicate his pre-occupation.)*

LORD LOAM. Eh?

ERNEST. Silence, if you please. *(He ponders.)*

LORD LOAM. I have been thinking that I ought to give you my boots.

ERNEST *(turning sharply)*. What!

LADY MARY. Father!

LORD LOAM *(genially)*. Take them, my boy. *(He holds out his feet—*ERNEST *eagerly pulls off boots and puts them on. The* GIRLS *cannot understand.)* I daresay you want to know why I give them to you, Ernest?

ERNEST. Not at all. The great thing is I've got 'em, I've got 'em. *(He stamps up* C., *triumphantly.)*

LORD LOAM *(rising and moving up* R.C. *and back to* ERNEST. *Business of thorn in his foot)*. My reason is that as head of this little party— *(He gives the* GIRLS *a knowing look.)* You, Ernest, shall be our hunter, you shall clear the forests of those savage beasts that make them so dangerous. *(Pleasantly.)* And now you know, my dear nephew, why I have given you my boots. *(He moves away up* R.C.)

ERNEST. This is my answer. *(He kicks off the boots, flings them to* LORD LOAM, *crosses to* L. *and puts on his pumps again.)*

(LADY AGATHA *creeps round, snatches the boots and crosses up* C. *and off behind the hut.)*

LADY MARY. Father, assert yourself.

LORD LOAM. I shall now assert myself. *(He crosses above the bucket to* C., *but does not know what to do.)* Call Crichton.

LADY MARY *(going to his* R.). Oh, Father!

LADY CATHERINE *(moves up* R., *calling)*. Crichton! *(He moves down* R. *again.)*

(CRICHTON *enters from behind the hut up* R., *and crosses to below and* R. *of the fire.)*

ERNEST *(standing* L.C.). Crichton, look here——

LORD LOAM. Silence! Crichton, I want your advice as to what I ought to do with Mr. Ernest. He has defied me.

ERNEST *(moves towards* LORD LOAM). Pooh!

CRICHTON. May I speak openly, my lord?

LADY MARY *(boldly and significantly at* R. *of* LORD LOAM). That is what we desire.

CRICHTON. Then I may say, your lordship, that I have been considering Mr. Ernest's case at odd moments for the last two days.

ERNEST. My case?

CRICHTON. Since we landed on the island, my lord, it seems to me that Mr. Ernest's epigrams have been particularly brilliant.

ERNEST *(gratified)*. Thank you, Crichton.

CRICHTON. But I find—I seem to find it growing wild, my lord, in the woods, that sayings which might be justly admired in England are not much use on an island. I would therefore most respectfully propose that henchforth every time Mr. Ernest favours us with one of his eqigrams his head should be immersed in a bucket of cold spring water.

LORD LOAM. Serve him right.

ERNEST *(crosses up to* L. *of* LORD LOAM). I should like to see you try to do it, Uncle.

CRICHTON. My feeling, my lord, is that at the next offense, I should conduct him to a retired spot, where I shall proceed to carry out the undertaking in as respectful a manner as is consistent with a thorough immersion. *(His manner, though quiet, is firm—he evidently means what he says.)*

LADY MARY. Father, you must not permit this. Ernest is your nephew.

LORD LOAM *(seeing the point)*. After all, he is my nephew, Crichton, and as I am sure he now sees that I am a strong man——

ERNEST *(stepping a pace nearer to* LORD LOAM). A strong man! You! You mean a stout man, Uncle. You are one of mind to two of matter. Ha, ha! (LORD LOAM *turns to* LADY MARY. ERNEST *smiles on seeing he has said a good thing, then starts as he observes that* CRICHTON *is quietly pulling up his sleeves.* ERNEST *is alarmed and backs to* L. LORD LOAM *makes no movement.* CRICHTON *walks towards* ERNEST. ERNEST *addresses* CRICHTON *with feeble firmness.*) Sit down, sir.

CRICHTON (*in the tone of one not to be trifled with*). Is it to be before the ladies, Mr. Ernest, or in the privacy of the wood? (*He fixes* ERNEST *with his eye.* ERNEST *is cowed.*) Come! (*He crosses up* C., *and turns.*) Come!

ERNEST (*affecting bravado*). Oh, all right! (*He moves* C.) I don't care!

CRICHTON (*as* ERNEST *reaches the bucket*). Bring that bucket.

(*He crosses up* C *and off* R. *behind the hut, followed by* ERNEST, *who takes the bucket.* TREHERNE *has come down to* LADY CATHERINE R.)

LORD LOAM (*following them up* C., *then turning back to* C.). I'm sorry for him, but I had to be firm.

LADY MARY (*distressed*). Oh, Father, it wasn't you who was firm. Crichton did it himself.

LORD LOAM. Bless me—so he did.

LADY MARY (*crosses up to him* C.). Father, be strong.

LORD LOAM. You can't mean that my faithful Crichton——

LADY MARY (*crossing below and to* L. *of* LORD LOAM). Yes, I do.

TREHERNE (*coming to up* R.C.). Lady Mary, I stake my work that Crichton is incapable of acting dishonourably.

LADY MARY (*puzzled, yet with conviction—crossing to* L. *of the tripod, resting one hand on it*). I know that —I know it as well as you. Don't you see that that is what makes him so dangerous?

TREHERNE. By Jove—I—I believe I catch your meaning.

LADY CATHERINE (going up R. and looking off). He is coming back.

LORD LOAM (struck with the idea). Then let us all go into the hut. (LADY MARY hands him his sou'wester which he took off and put by the bucket.) Just to show him at once that it is our hut.

(He crosses up C. and towards R., followed by LADY MARY and LADY CATHERINE. LADY CATHERINE enters the hut and stands at the window, LORD LOAM and LADY MARY remain at the door, TREHERNE gets on the roof.)

LADY MARY. Father, I implore you, assert yourself now and for ever.

LORD LOAM. I will.

LADY MARY. And please don't ask him how you are to do it.

LORD LOAM. Mary! (CRICHTON enters from up R., at C., and crosses to L. of the tripod, kneeling at it.) Have you carried out my instructions, Crichton?

CRICHTON (putting sticks on the fire). Yes, my lord.

(Enter ERNEST with the bucket from up R., at C., leaves it by the hut, crosses up and sits on the rocks L. LADY AGATHA follows him on and sits beside him, and helps to dry his head with palm leaves, etc.)

LADY AGATHA. It's infamous!

LORD LOAM. My orders, Agatha!

LADY MARY (encouraging him). Father!

LORD LOAM. Before I give you further orders, Crichton——

CRICHTON. Yes, my lord. (He rises, moves L., picking up twigs for the fire.)

LORD LOAM (delighted—to the OTHERS). Pooh! It's all right.

LADY MARY. No.

LORD LOAM (*crossing to* L.C., *followed by* LADY MARY, *on his* R.). Well, well! This question of leadership—what do you think now?

CRICHTON. My lord, I feel it is a matter with which I have nothing to do. (*He moves down* L. *for more wood.*)

LORD LOAM. Excellent! Mary! That settles it, I think.

LADY MARY. It seems to, but——

CRICHTON (*below the rocks* L., *picking up twigs*). It will settle itself naturally, my lord, without any interference from us.

(*The* OTHERS *exchange disturbed glances, turning to each other, very concerned.*)

LADY MARY. Father!

LORD LOAM (*crosses down* L.C.). It settled itself long ago, Crichton, when I was born a peer, and you, for instance, were born a servant.

CRICHTON. Yes, your lordship, that was how it all came about quite naturally in England. We had nothing to do with it there and we shall have as little to do with it here. (*He crosses* LORD LOAM *to* R. *of the fire, after breaking a twig on his knee.*)

TREHERNE (*relieved, on the roof*). That's all right.

(CRICHTON *is about to kneel.*)

LADY MARY. One moment. (*She crosses to the tripod and puts her hand on it.*) In short, Crichton, his lordship will continue to be our natural head.

CRICHTON. I daresay, my lady; I daresay. (*Kneeling.*)

LADY CATHERINE (*through the window*). But you must *know.*

CRICHTON (*turning to face her*). Asking your pardon, my lady, one can't be sure—on an island.

(LADY MARY *moves to* LORD LOAM, *encouraging him to speak.*)

LORD LOAM. Crichton, I don't like this.

CRICHTON (R.C., *rising.*) The more I think of it, your lordship, the more uneasy I become. When I heard, my lord, that you had left that hairpin behind—— *(He shakes his head.)*

(LADY CATHERINE *has come out of the hut.* LADY AGATHA *is standing on the lower edge of the rock, above and to* R. *of* ERNEST.)

LORD LOAM. One hairpin among so many would only have caused dissension.

CRICHTON. Not so, my lord. From one hairpin we could have made a needle—with that needle we could out of the skins have sewn trousers of which your lordship is very much in need. *(He kneels again.)* Indeed, we are all of us in need of them.

ALL. All!

(LADY CATHERINE *moves to* R. *of* LADY MARY *at* L.C.; LADY AGATHA *jumps down and comes on* LADY MARY'S L., *who puts protecting arms around them.*)

CRICHTON. On an island, my lady.

LADY AGATHA. Father!

(TREHERNE *jumps off the roof and stands down* R.)

CRICHTON *(in agony).* My lady! If nature does not think them necessary you may be quite sure she will not ask you to wear them. But among all this undergrowth——

LADY MARY *(coming down* L. *and turning to face the* OTHERS) Now you see this man in his true colours.

LORD LOAM. Crichton, you will either this moment say "Down with nature" or——

CRICHTON *(scandalized).* My lord!

LORD LOAM *(loftily).* Then this is my last word to you—take a month's notice.

(The sound of the sea is heard again. LORD LOAM *motions his daughters, who, in silence, file into the hut,* LADY CATHERINE *first,* LADY AGATHA *second,* LADY MARY *third.* LADY MARY *goes to the window.* LORD LOAM *follows and stands at the door.* ERNEST *is now sitting on a high rock* L.)

CRICHTON *(in great distress—crosses up to* L.C.). Your lordship, the disgrace—— *(He turns to face* R.)

(The sea effect continues until the end of the Act.)

LORD LOAM *(as if to bar his entrance to the hut).* Not another word—you may go.

LADY MARY *(through the window).* And don't come to me, Crichton, for a character.

ERNEST. Aren't you all forgetting that this is an island?

(They are ALL *taken back.* LORD LOAM, *at a loss, turns to* LADY MARY *for aid.)*

LADY MARY *(coming out of the hut to* C.). It makes only this difference—that you may go at once, Crichton, to some other part of the island.

*(*CRICHTON *moves back to down* R. *in silence, drops the twigs, then turns and takes off his hat. The scene has become slowly darker, the sunset tints fading.)*

CRICHTON. My lady, let me work for you.

LORD LOAM. Go!

CRICHTON *(moving up* R.C.). You need me, you need me sorely, my lord. *(They* ALL *look at* CRICHTON, *then at* LADY MARY.) I—I can't desert you—I won't!

LADY MARY *(moving down* L.C.). Then, Father, there is but one alternative, *we* must leave him.

(CRICHTON *comes slowly down to* L. *of the tripod.*)

TREHERNE (*moving in a little* R.C.). It seems a pity.
LADY CATHERINE (*through the window—to* TRE-
HERNE). *You* will work for us.
TREHERNE. Most willingly. But I must warn you all
that so far Crichton has done nine-tenths of the scoring.
I have only managed to help him by keeping my end
up.
LADY MARY (*a pace nearer* C.). The question is—
are we to leave this man?
LORD LOAM (*crossing to the rocks* L.). Come, my
dears.

(LADY CATHERINE *and* LADY AGATHA, *with the boots
under her arm, follow, to the rocks.*)

CRICHTON (*turning to face them*). My lord!
LORD LOAM. Mr. Treherne—Ernest—get our things.

(*They hesitate.*)

ERNEST (*coming down to a lower ledge of rock*). We
—haven't any, Uncle. They all belong to Crichton.
TREHERNE (*above and* R. *of the tripod*). Everything
we have he brought from the wreck—he went back to it
before it sank. He risked his life.
CRICHTON. Take them, my lord, anything you would
care for is yours.

(LORD LOAM *is about to speak.*)

LADY MARY (*sharply, stops her father*). Nothing.
ERNEST. Rot! If I could have your socks, Crich-
ton—— (*Coming down* L. *a little.*)
LADY MARY. Nothing! Father, we are ready.

(LORD LOAM *moves up the rocks, followed by the*
GIRLS.)

CRICHTON *(moving to* C.*)*. My lord, I implore you—
I am not desirous of being head. You have a try at it,
my lord.

LORD LOAM. A try at it!

CRICHTON. It may be that you will prove the best
man——

LORD LOAM. Maybe! Come, my children!

(They exit L.*, up the rocks.)*

TREHERNE *(going after the* OTHERS, *but turning up*
L.C.*)*. Crichton, I'm sorry, but, of course, I must go
with them.

(The moonlight is now rising.)

CRICHTON. Certainly, sir! One moment. *(He turns a
little down* R.C. *and calls.)* Tweeny! (TWEENY *enters
down* R., *and he takes her hand.)* Will you be so kind
as to take her to the others?

TREHERNE. Assuredly.

TWEENY. But what do it all mean?

CRICHTON. Does, Tweeny; does. *(He kindly passes
her over towards* TREHERNE.*)* We shall meet again
soon, Tweeny. Good night.

*(*TREHERNE *helps her up the rocks and she exits.)*

TREHERNE *(turning on the lower ledge of rock)*.
Good night. I daresay they are not far away.

CRICHTON. They went westward, sir, and the wind
is blowing in that direction.

TREHERNE. Why, what does that matter?

CRICHTON. It may mean, sir, that Nature is already
taking the matter into her own hands. They are all
hungry, sir. The wind is blowing westward and—*(he
lifts the lid)* and that pot is full of Nature, full of
Nature, Mr. Treherne. Good night, sir.

*(The scene has become very dark, but soon the moon-
    light is brighter, casting a pool of light around the
    fire and the hut.)*

TREHERNE. Good night.

He exits L. CRICHTON *stirs the pot again and puts twigs
    on the fire. The growl of a beast is heard off* L.
    CRICHTON *picks up the cutlass and looks cautiously
    in that direction, moving across* L. *to the long
    grass. Then he backs carefully to* C., *and lays the
    cutlass down. Moving to the fire, he takes out his
    pipe, and fills it with tobacco from various pockets,
    and lights it from the fire. The leaves rustle. He
    stirs the pot, replaces the lid, and sits above the
    fire smoking patiently. Presently,* ERNEST *and*
    LADY AGATHA *re-enter* L., *down the rocks, fol-
    lowed by* LORD LOAM, *and then* TWEENY. *A
    moment later,* TREHERNE *follows with* LADY
    CATHERINE. *They* ALL *move, a trifle shamefaced,
    across above the fire and sit in a group around it.*
    CRICHTON *has not moved. He is gazing out front,
    and smoking. The last to arrive is* LADY MARY,
    who seats herself on the lowest ledge of the rocks
    L.C., *and hides her face in her hands, and cries.
    Only then does* CRICHTON *turn his head to look
    at her as—*

The CURTAIN *falls.*

ACT III

SCENE.—*The hall of their island home, two years later.*
The walls and roof are of stout logs. Across the joists supporting the roof are implements such as spades, etc., all home made. From hooks hang cured hams, etc. Heads of tiger-cats and other animals ornament the walls, and on the wooden floor are several skins.

The back wall, as to the R. section, is somewhat angled and contains a long low window and a small but higher one at about C.

(See the Ground Plan.)

The L. section of the back wall shows a deep recess which is the kitchen. In the centre of this is the fireplace, a section of an old boat serving as a chimney. R. of the fire, a small table, stool and a drying rack. L. of the fire, a small sink and another stool. Folding screens at either side enable this apartment to be shut off from the rest. The R. screen has a serving-hatch at about shoulder height.

To L. of the kitchen is an opening which leads on to a passage to other rooms. There are other doors down R. and L. respectively.

R.C., a wooden settee, home made. C., an armchair which may be home made or salvaged from the wreck. At L.C., a rough wooden table to seat six persons. Above, below and at either side are roughly made stools, their seats square or triangular but revealing their source of manufacture.

There is a dresser at L., a small table at R., a low bench or chest below the window up R.C., another

75

stool or so, and below the small window up C., *a contraption like the spokes of a steering-wheel without the rim, set in a frame. This is the lever which will set off the beacon lights.*

The general effect is romantic but quite barbaric.

The time is late afternoon, or early evening, but there is plenty of sunshine streaming into the room.

When the CURTAIN *rises,* TWEENY *is seated on the settee at* R.C., *singing, and plucking the feathers of an armadillo bird and dropping them on to a cloth spread on the floor. She is dressed in her maid's dress, carefully mended, though with many patches. Outside, an unseen person whistles as if to draw her attention. She turns her head and then resumes her work and singing. The whistler now appears at the long window. It is* LORD LOAM, *wearing clothes of leather. He looks into the room cautiously and then whistles to* TWEENY *in the manner of an English policeman whistling to a cook. There is no response.*

LORD LOAM. Tweeny!

TWEENY (*without looking round*). Get away with you!

(LORD LOAM *climbs in through the window opening. He is carrying a home-made concertina. He is now the handy man about the house, but happy and in gay spirit. He dances down to* C., *and then up* L.C., *playing his concertina and singing:*)

LORD LOAM. I'm a chicketty chicketty chick chick! Chicketty Chicketty chee! (*Dancing down* L.C. *and up*). I'm a chicketty chicketty chick chick—chicketty, chicketty chee— (*He stops as a buzzing is heard and a hand-printed card appears in the passage opening up* L., *with the words* "SILENCE" *on it.* LORD LOAM *is*

cowed, and turns to TWEENY, *who laughs.)* I thought
the Gov. was out!

(He crosses quickly to L., *and puts the concertina on
the stool below the dresser, and returns to* C. *During this,* TWEENY *rises and puts the bird on the
seat* R.C., *crosses to the table, opens the drawer,
takes out a table napkin and begins to set the table.*
LORD LOAM, *seeing this, goes* R.C. *and takes up the
task of plucking the bird.)*

TWEENY *(during the above).* Well, you see he ain't.
Iɪ he was to catch you here idling—
LORD LOAM *(hastily commencing to pluck the bird—
cautiously).* What is he doing now?
TWEENY *(spreading a cloth on the table).* I think
he's working out that plan for the hot and cold. *(She
gets two knives, forks, spoons and goblets, and sets
them at the top end of the table evidently for one person.)*
LORD LOAM *(enthusiastic).* And he'll manage it too!
The man who could build a blacksmith's forge without
tools——
TWEENY. He made the tools. *(She is now finishing
the business at the table.)*
LORD LOAM. Out of half a dozen rusty nails. The
saw-mill, Tweeny, the speaking tube—the electric lighting—and look at the use he has made of the bits of the
yacht that were washed ashore *(pointing to boat and
settee* R.*)*, and all in two years. He's a master I'm
proud to pluck for.

(He hums happily that he's a chicketty chick. TWEENY
crosses to him and looks at him in wonder.)

TWEENY. Daddy, you're of little use, but you're a
bright cheerful creature for to have about the house.
*(*LORD LOAM *hums on, beaming at her. A slight pause.
Getting a stool from* R. *of the table and sitting* R. *of*

LORD LOAM. *Curiously.)* Do you ever think—of old
times now? (LORD LOAM *pulls his hand across his eyes
in a dazed way.)* We was all a bit different then.

LORD LOAM *(heavily).* Circumstances alter cases.
(He resumes the plucking contentedly.)

TWEENY. But, Daddy, if the chance was to come of
getting back?

LORD LOAM *(contentedly).* I have given up bothering
about it.

TWEENY. You bothered that day, long ago, when we
saw a ship passing the island. How we all ran like
crazy folk into the water, Daddy, and screamed and
held out our arms! *(They* BOTH *hold out their arms to
an imaginary ship, a little agitated.)* But it sailed away
and we never seen another.

LORD LOAM. If we had had that electric contrivance
we have now, we could have attracted that ship's notice.
(Looking at the apparatus above the door R.) A touch
on that lever, Tweeny—— *(He points to it. She rises,
crosses round to* R.C., *and gazes at it in wonder.)* and
in a few moments bonfires would be blazing all round
the shore.

TWEENY *(almost touching the apparatus, then backing away).* It's the most wonderful thing he has done.
(She sits on the L. *end of the seat* R.)

LORD LOAM. And then—England—home! *(He is
picturing it in his mind.)*

TWEENY *(also seeing visions).* London of a Satur-
day night!

LORD LOAM *(feeling himself in the Upper House—
puts bird down—rises).* My lords, in rising once more
to address this historic chamber—I feel that——

TWEENY. There was a little ham and beef shop in
the Old Kent Road—as I used to go to——

(LORD LOAM *shakes off these visions.)*

LORD LOAM *(crossing to* R. *of the chair* C. *Ingratiat-*

ingly). Tweeny, do you think I could have an egg to my tea?

(ERNEST *enters at the window* R.C., *also in leather, carrying two pails suspended by a pole on his shoulder after the rustic fashion—one is the bucket, the other a large tree bark covered with skins.*)

ERNEST (*standing on the window-ledge*). What is that about an egg? Why should you have an egg?

LORD LOAM (*with hauteur*). That's my affair. (*He crosses above the table to* L. *and down.*) I—I—— (*Over his shoulder at the door* L.) The Gov. has never put *my* head in a bucket.

(*He exits conceitedly* L. ERNEST *comes down into the room and puts the buckets down up* C. TWEENY *rises, crosses* L. *and puts the lamp on the lower* L. *end of the table. She then moves the stool* L.C. *back to the* R. *edge of the table.*)

ERNEST (*during the above*). Nor mine for nearly three months. It was only last week, Tweeny, that he said to me, "Ernest, the water cure has worked marvels in you, and I question whether I shall require to dip you any more." (*Complacently.*) Now you know, that sort of thing encourages a fellow.

(*He moves below the chair* C. *to* R.C. TWEENY *crosses above the table to* L. *of the chair.*)

TWEENY. I will say, Erny, I never seen a young chap more improved.

ERNEST (*turning, at* R.C., *gratified*). Thank you, Tweeny—that's very precious to me.

TWEENY. Oh, go on.

(*She crosses up to kitchen and works the bellows, poking the fire. During the following scene she moves a stool that is* L. *of the hearth down stage, makes three slices of toast, puts them in a toast-*

rack, crosses to the sink and gets a large and a small shell and starts wiping them with a dish-cloth. This business takes her from the time she goes up until ERNEST *comes and speaks to her later.* TREHERNE *enters down* L. *carrying a small box. He sees* ERNEST *and crosses sideways, trying to hide it—crosses to* R.)

ERNEST *(to below the chair* C.). What have you got there, John?

TREHERNE *(coming to* ERNEST *above and to* L. *of the chair).* Don't tell anybody. It is a little present for the Gov.—a set of razors. One for each day in the week. *(He opens the box and takes one out.)*

ERNEST. Shells! He'll like that. He likes sets of things.

TREHERNE. Have *you* noticed that?

ERNEST. Rather.

TREHERNE *(down level with* ERNEST). He's becoming a bit magnificent in his ideas.

ERNEST. John, it sometimes gives me the creeps.

TREHERNE *(after a glance up* L., *over his shoulder).* What do you think of that brilliant robe he got the girls to make for him?

ERNEST *(leaning on* TREHERNE'S R. *shoulder, confidentally).* I think he looks too regal in it.

TREHERNE. Yes, but I sometimes fancy that that's why he's so fond of wearing it. *(He closes the box and crosses* R.) Well, I must take these down to the grindstone and put an edge on them.

(He exits, re-appearing outside the long window a moment later.)

ERNEST *(going up to the window).* I say, John, I want a word with you.

TREHERNE *(stops,* R. *of* ERNEST). Well?

ERNEST *(in some confusion).* Dash it all—*(he sits on the window-sill)*—you know you're a parson.

TREHERNE *(leaning over the sill).* One of the best

things the Gov. has done is to insist that none of you forget it.

ERNEST (*looking up at* TREHERNE). Then—would you—John?

TREHERNE. What?

ERNEST. Officiate at a marriage ceremony, John?

TREHERNE (*straightening up, surprised*). Now that's really odd.

(*He climbs back into the room and sits on the window-sill, R. of* ERNEST.)

ERNEST. Seems to me it's very natural. And if it's natural, John, it's right.

TREHERNE. I mean, that same question has been put to me to-day already.

ERNEST (*eagerly*). By one of the women?

TREHERNE. Oh no! They all put it to me long ago! This time it was by the Gov. himself.

ERNEST. By Jove! (*Admiringly.*) I say, John, what an observant beggar he is!

TRENERNE. Ah! You fancy he was thinking of you?

ERNEST. I do not hesitate to affirm, John, that he has seen the lovelight in my eyes. You answered——?

TREHERNE. I said yes, I thought it would be my duty to officiate if called upon.

ERNEST. You're a brick.

TREHERNE. But I wonder whether he was thinking of you?

ERNEST. Make your mind easy about that.

TREHERNE. Well, well. Agatha is a very fine girl.

ERNEST. Agatha? What made you think it was Agatha?

TREHERNE. Man alive, you told me all about it soon after we were wrecked.

ERNEST. Pooh! (*He rises and crosses to* C.) Agatha's all very well, John, but I'm flying at bigger game.

TREHERNE (*following him down on his* R.). Ernest, which is it?

ERNEST (*down* L. *of and below the* C. *chair*). Tweeny, of course.

TREHERNE. Tweeny! (*After a glance up to the kitchen. Reprovingly.*) Ernest, I hope her cooking has nothing to do with this.

ERNEST. Her cooking has very little to do with it, although her light pastry, eh, John?

(*They* BOTH *show their appreciation of it.*)

TREHERNE. But does she return your affection?

ERNEST. Yes, John, I believe I may say so—I am unworthy of her, but I think I have touched her heart.

TREHERNE. Some people seem to have all the luck. As you know, Catherine won't look at me.

ERNEST. I'm sorry, John.

TREHERNE. It's my desert, I'm a second-rater—— (*He offers his hand, which* ERNEST *grasps.*) Well, my heartiest good wishes, Ernest. (*He crosses to the door* R.)

ERNEST (*to* R. *of the chair* C.). How's the little black pig to-day?

TREHERNE (*turning at the door*). He's begun to eat again. (*He exits* R. *and is seen disappearing beyond the window.*)

ERNEST (*turning a little up* C.). Are you very busy, Tweeny?

TWEENY (*in the kitchen,* L. *end, cleaning shells*). There's always work to do, but if you want me, Ernest——

ERNEST (*turning to face her*). There's something I should like to say to you if you don't mind listening.

TWEENY (*good-naturedly*). Willingly. (*She comes down with her work and sits on a stool,* R. *of the table* L.C.)

ERNEST (*coming slowly down on her* R., *above her*). What an ass I used to be, Tweeny.

TWEENY (*cleaning the shell briskly.*) Oh, let bygones be bygones,

ERNEST *(fingering the chair* C., *uncertainly).* I'm no great shakes even now.

TWEENY. We all like you, Ernest—you're so willing, and it was you as made that seat.

ERNEST *(glancing at the seat* R.). It might have been better made.

TWEENY. The Gov. says every one has a gift, and that yours is for carpentering.

ERNEST *(coming down level with her).* I don't say it's a bad seat, but I could make a better. Tweeny, I should like to make some more chairs—and a table—and a tablecloth—and some knives and forks. I have an idea for a sideboard.

(TWEENY puts the shells and the cloth on the floor, and bends down to tie up a thong of her boot.)

TWEENY *(business).* I like to hear you. But we're pretty full now— *(pulling at the thong)* —have you thought where we could put them?

ERNEST. Yes. There's that sunny little glade near Porcupine Stream.

TWEENY *(looking up at him).* You would put them *there?*

ERNEST. It's a homely spot.

TWEENY *(she lifts her leg and continues tying her thong).* But in the open!

ERNEST. I would build a little house round them, Tweeny—and when it was built, I would go with my hat in my hand to a girl I know, and I would say to her —*(he kneels on her* L.)—"I was an ass when you knew me first, and I'm no great shakes even now, but I love you truly, Tweeny, won't you come to my little house?"

TWEENY *(rising).* Oh, Ernest, I wasn't understanding. It's good of you—but I must say—no!

ERNEST. I feared it would be no. *(He rises.)*

TWEENY. I'm that sorry. *(She turns to him.)*

ERNEST *(bravely).* Thank you, Tweeny—it can't be helped. *(He turns and goes up* R.C.)

TWEENY. No! *(She goes down L. and covers up the parrot.)*

ERNEST *(turning and crossing back to above the table L.C.).* Tweeny, we shall be disappointing the Gov.

TWEENY *(turning).* What's that?

ERNEST. He wanted us to marry.

TWEENY *(half dazed).* You and me, the Gov.! *(She turns to dresser and buries her face in her hands with grief.* ERNEST *sighs heavily and leans on the table L.C. Someone is heard outside, drawing near, singing a gay tune. She starts up fiercely.)* That's her, that's the thing what stole his heart from me! *(She crosses up C., to L. of the small window.)*

(The whistler, who proves to be LADY MARY, appears at the window. She is dressed in picturesque boy's garments of thin leather, feather leaves, etc., etc., and carries bow and arrows, and has a slain buck and a couple of ducks.)

LADY MARY *(holding up the buck).* Victory!

(TWEENY turns away sourly, comes down to R. of the chair and picks up the bird and the cloth. LADY MARY throws down the buck outside, and jumps in through the window, and throws down her hat on the seat R.)

TWEENY *(turning up C.).* Drat you, Polly—why don't you wipe your feet?

LADY MARY *(R.C., good-naturedly).* Come, Tweeny, be nice to me. *(Giving her a hug.)* It's a splendid buck.

(TWEENY shakes her off, goes up into the kitchen, with the bird. LADY MARY throws the ducks on the small table R. and takes the bow and quiver off her shoulder.)

ERNEST *(coming down R. of the table L.C.).* Where

did you get it? *(He sits on the L. side of the table, lower end.)*

LADY MARY *(moving across above the seat R., to C.).* I sighted a herd near Penguin's Creek, but had to creep round Silver Lake to get windward of them. *(She hangs the bow and quiver up on a hook between the windows, standing on a stool.)* However, they spotted me and then the fun began. *(She jumps down, crosses R. for ducks, crosses again and sits on a stool facing ERNEST, pulling it out from the table.)* There was nothing for it but to try and run them down, so I singled out a fat buck and away we went down the shore of the lake, up the valley of rolling stones, he doubled into Brawling River and took to the water, but I swam after him—the river is only half a mile broad there, but it runs strong. He went spinning down the rapids—down I went in pursuit—he clambered ashore, I clambered ashore—away we tore helter-skelter up the hill and down again. I lost him in the marshes, got on his track again near Bread Fruit Wood, and brought him down with an arrow in Fire-fly Grove.

(TWEENY has gradually come down and stands between ERNEST and MARY—half sitting on the table L.C.)

TWEENY. Ain't you tired?
LADY MARY. Tired? *(She rises.)* It was gorgeous.

(She crosses R., whistling, picks up the ducks and hangs them on the first hook. ERNEST rises and crosses up to the window R.C.)

TWEENY *(moving to C.).* I can't abide a woman whistling.

LADY MARY *(jumps down).* Can't you? I like it. *(She whistles.)*

TWEENEY. Drop it, Polly, I tell you!

LADY MARY *(crossing to TWEENY).* I won't. I'm as good as you are.

(They face each other defiantly. LADY MARY *goes towards* TWEENY, *whistling.)*

TWEENY. Now, Polly, what do yer want to be so aggravating for? Drop it, I tell yer.

ERNEST *(turning).* I say! I say! Is this necessary? Think how it would pain *him.*

(LADY MARY *looks at the door* L.C.)

LADY MARY *(contritely).* Tweeny, I beg your pardon. If my whistling annoys you, I shall try to cure myself of it. (ERNEST *returns to the kitchen and sits on the stool* R. *of the hearth. To* LADY MARY'S *surprise* TWEENY *bursts into tears, crosses and sits on the stool* R. *of the table* L.C. *Crossing and sitting on the* L. *arm of the chair* C.) Why, how can that hurt you, Tweeny dear?

TWEENY. Because I can't make you lose your temper!

LADY MARY. Indeed, I often do—would that I were nicer to everybody.

TWEENY. There yer go again. What makes yer want to be so nice, Polly?

LADY MARY *(fervently).* Only thankfulness, Tweeny. *(She throws herself back in the armchair.)* It's such fun to be alive.

(A wild cry is heard outside, then LADY CATHERINE *runs to the window and stands with one foot on the ledge, holding in her right hand a rod, and in her left hand some fish. She is in boy's clothes.)*

LADY CATHERINE. We've got some ripping fish for the Gov's dinner. Are we in time? We ran all the way.

TWEENY *(rising and crossing up* R.C.). You'll please to cook them yourself, Kitty, and look sharp about it. *(She puts the stool up* C. *back in the kitchen, also picks up the two shells and cloth, and works the bellows.)*

LADY CATHERINE. Rather. *(She jumps into the room.)*

(At the same moment another wild cry is heard and LADY AGATHA enters by the door down R. and running to C. shows her fish to LADY MARY. LADY CATHERINE takes her rod and LADY AGATHA's and puts them above the dresser L.)

LADY AGATHA *(calling)*. Has the Gov. decided who is to wait on him to-day?

LADY CATHERINE *(crossing to the sink in the kitchen with the fish and starting to clean them)*. It's my turn.

LADY AGATHA *(going up to below the R. side of the kitchen)*. I don't see that.

(TWEENY puts down the bellows and turns.)

TWEENY *(bitterly—between them)*. It's to be neither of you, Aggy, he wants Polly again.

(LADY MARY, with a joyous laugh, rises, and crosses up to above the seat R.C.)

LADY AGATHA *(coming to her)*. Polly, you toad——

(LADY MARY laughs all the more, and flips her fingers in LADY AGATHA's face. LADY AGATHA crosses and throws herself full length on the couch.)

TWEENY *(coming down towards MARY C.)*. How dare you look so happy?

LADY MARY. Tweeny. *(Trying to embrace her, but TWEENY throws her off.)* If there was anything I could do to make you happy also.

TWEENY. Me? *(Recklessly.)* Oh, I'm so happy—— *(She comes down to R. of the table L.C.)*. I've just had a proposal, I tell you.

(LADY MARY comes down a little, anxiously.)

LADY AGATHA *(jumping up)*. A proposal?

LADY CATHERINE *(coming down to* C., *with the fish, points at* CRICHTON'S *direction)*. Not—not——

(ERNEST *rises.*)

ERNEST *(coming to the* R. *corner of the kitchen)*. You needn't be alarmed, it's only me.

(The SISTERS *turn to look up at him.* TWEENY *faces down stage.)*

LADY MARY. Was it you, Ernest? *(She crosses to the passage up* L. *and looks off, then moving to* L.C.)

LADY AGATHA *(moving up* R.C.). Ernest, you dear—I got such a shock. *(She crosses back to the window, jumps up on the sill and picks flowers for the table.)*

LADY CATHERINE. It was only Ernest. *(Showing him the fish.)* They are beautifully fresh—come and help me to cook them. *(She returns to the sink, singing.)*

ERNEST *(looking round and seeing that not one of the four women is taking any notice of him)*. I think you might all be a little sorry for a chap. *(He crosses to* L. *of* LADY AGATHA.) I'm particularly disappointed in you, Aggy. Seeing that I was half engaged to you, I think you might have the good feeling to be a little more hurt.

LADY AGATHA. Oh bother! *(Picking flowers.)*

ERNEST *(coming* C. *and looking round once more—then crossing down to the door* L. *and turning)*. I shall now go and lie down for a bit.

(He exits L. TWEENY *moves to* R. *of the lower end of the table.)*

LADY MARY *(coming to* L. *of* TWEENY, *appealingly.)* Tweeny, as the Gov. has chosen me to wait on him, may I have the loan of—*(she picks up* TWEENY'S *skirt)* it again?

TWEENY (*vindictively—dragging her skirt away*). No, you mayn't. (*Backing up stage.*)

LADY AGATHA (*jumps down from the window-sill, crosses and nudges* TWEENY). Don't you give it to her. (*She crosses to the dresser for a vessel, then up to the sink for water, crosses to L. of the table again and puts the flowers on it during the following lines.*)

TWEENY (*backing to* C.). It's mine.

LADY MARY (*following* TWEENY *up*). You know quite well that he prefers to be waited on in a skirt.

TWEENY. I don't care. (*She replaces the stool by the table* L.C.) Get one for yourself.

(*She turns* R., *but* LADY MARY *follows.*)

LADY MARY (*puts her hand on* TWEENY'S *shoulder and turns her round*). It is the only one on the island.

TWEENY (*throwing her off*). And it's mine.

(*She backs up* C., *and* LADY MARY *follows.* LADY CATHERINE *comes down* C. LADY AGATHA *crosses round below the table to* L.C.)

LADY MARY (*getting in front of her up* C., *threateningly*). Tweeny, give me that skirt directly!

LADY CATHERINE. Don't.

(LADY CATHERINE *and* LADY AGATHA *egg* TWEENY *on, with signs and gestures, behind* LADY MARY'S *back.*)

TWEENY. I shan't.

(LADY MARY *advances on* TWEENY *pugnaciously, their tongues are between their teeth after the manner of women about to struggle—*LADY AGATHA *is backing* TWEENY.)

LADY MARY. I shall make you.

TWEENY. Like to see you try.

(Buzzer and sign.

They have become loud and speak simultaneously with "Oh's" and "Ah's"—suddenly the buzzing is heard and a card appears with the inscription: "DOGS DELIGHT TO BARK AND BITE." ALL stop, startled. LADY MARY crosses to the dresser for the wreath of green leaves and then down L. to the glass, puts it on, LADY CATHERINE crosses to the sink again, puts the fish down and then to above the table with the toast on a shell and puts it in toast-rack. LADY AGATHA crosses to L. of the table, gets the menu from the dresser and puts it on the R. side of the table. LADY MARY crosses below the table to up R.C. TWEENY crosses up to the bellows, then comes down a few steps and looks at LADY CATHERINE and LADY AGATHA. They nod that they are ready. LADY CATHERINE crosses up and closes the R. door. LADY AGATHA closes the L. door. TWEENY also retires into the kitchen. LADY MARY crosses to see that the table is right—throws a flower away and puts the one she is wearing in its place,—sounds tom-tom and replaces it, unloops the punkah and stands like a servant R. of the entrance up L.)

(NOTE.—*A serving-hole is in the kitchen door for sending dishes through.)*

(CRICHTON *enters up L. from the passage with a book in his hand, crosses down L.C., looks at the table, moves to the chair, LADY MARY placing it for him. She goes to R. of the table and gets the menu, crosses round to L. of him, and hands it to him. He reads it.)*

CRICHTON. Clear, please. (LADY MARY *crosses up to the hatch, knocks, and* TWEENY *opens it.* LADY MARY *speaks to her, then* LADY CATHERINE *hands soup to* TWEENY *and she hands it to* LADY MARY. CRICHTON *puts a bnttonhole in his coat.* LADY MARY *crosses to* L. *of* CRICHTON *and puts the soup in front of him, and then goes up and works the punkah.* CRICHTON *takes a spoonful or two, puts the spoon down and takes a little salt, and then continues. When he puts his spoon down again,* LADY MARY *crosses to* L. *of him and removes his plate. He speaks without turning round.)* Excellent soup, Polly, but still a trifle too rich.

LADY MARY. Thank you.

(LADY MARY *takes the soup-plate up, and hands it to* TWEENY, *who gives her the fish, giving it a finishing touch with a little parsley. After putting it before* CRICHTON, LADY MARY *returns and works the punkah.* CRICHTON *nibbles the toast.)*

CRICHTON *(while eating).* Polly, you are a very smart girl.

LADY MARY *(bridling in servant manner).* La!

CRICHTON. And I'm not the first you've heard it from, I'll swear.

LADY MARY *(wriggling shoulders like a servant).* Oh, Gov.!

CRICHTON. Got any followers on the island, Polly?

LADY MARY *(tilting her nose).* Certainly not.

CRICHTON. I thought perhaps that John or Ernest——

LADY MARY *(wriggling conceitedly).* I don't say that it's for want of asking—— *(She crosses to down* L. *for a bottle and then up, above the table to* R. *of* CRICHTON.)

CRICHTON *(during the above—eating).* I'm very sure it isn't, Polly. *(A silence, in which he goes on eating.)* You may clear.

     (LADY MARY *crosses to* L. *of his chair.)*

LADY MARY. Thank *you.*

(She takes the fish plate away. CRICHTON *drinks, mean-*

while. LADY MARY *gets meat from* TWEENY *and a dish of vegetables, and crosses* L. *of* CRICHTON, *putting meat in front of him. She takes one of the spoons off the table and putting it in vegetable-dish, holds it for him to help himself, then puts the dish on the dresser, and returns to the punkah.*

CRICHTON *(eating).* Did you lose any arrows to-day?

LADY MARY. Only one—in Firefly Grove.

CRICHTON. You were as far as that? How did you get across the Black Gorge?

LADY MARY *(stops working the punkah).* I went across on the rope.

CRICHTON. Hand over hand?

LADY MARY. I wasn't in the least dizzy. *(She works the punkah.)*

CRICHTON *(moves).* Ah! You brave girl! *(He sits back, agitated over the peril she has been in.)* But you musn't do that again!

LADY MARY *(pouting, coming down* C. *a little).* It is such fun, Gov.

CRICHTON. I forbid it.

LADY MARY *(rebelling).* I shall! *(She stops working the punkah and throws the cord aside.)*

CRICHTON *(turns on her reprovingly).* Polly! Polly! Polly! *(He signs to her sternly to step forward—she holds back petulantly—he signs again, and she comes forward sulkily like a naughty child.)* Remember you must do as I say.

LADY MARY *(in a passion).* I shan't!

CRICHTON *(smiling at her fury).* We shall see. Frown at me, Polly—there—you do it at once. Clench your little fists, stamp your feet, bite your ribbons—— *(*LADY MARY *has begun to do all these things before he speaks, so that she seems to be doing his bidding. She is helpless, begins to cry—he is immediately kind.)* You child of Nature—was it cruel of me to wish to save you from harm? Are you angry with me because I couldn't——

LADY MARY *(drying her eyes)*. I'm an ungracious wretch. Oh, Gov., I don't try half enough to please you—I'm even wearing—when I know you prefer— *(indicating skirt in kitchen behind her)*—it.

CRICHTON. I admit I *do* prefer *it*. Perhaps I am a little old-fashioned in these matters. (LADY MARY *sobs.*) Ah, don't, Polly—that's nothing. I know very well that quite as many noble hearts beat in dual garments as in the dwelling-places of the great.

LADY MARY. If I could only please you, Gov.!

CRICHTON. Please me. *(He rises.)* You do please me, child, very much! Very much indeed. *(He sits again.)* No more, thank you.

(LADY MARY *crosses to L. of him, above the table, takes the plate and the vegetable-dish off the dresser, gives them through the aperture to* TWEENY, *crosses to L., gets the cruet tray, puts cruets, toast-rack, menu card on it and returns it to the dresser. She then gets a tray and scoop, and scoops the crumbs L. of the table. She then crosses to R., waits a moment like a servant as* CRICHTON'S *arm is in the way. He looks up and sees what she means, moves his arm and lets her finish. She then returns the tray to the dresser, gets fruit and a shell, and puts them in front of him. Having done this, she crosses R. of the table, pours out wine, then R. and turns on the switch of the table-lamp. She then crosses to L. of the table again, moves the lamp up towards* CRICHTON *and stands, as if washing her hands.)*

CRICHTON. Polly, there is only one thing about you that I don't quite like. (LADY MARY *looks up.*) That— action of the hands.

LADY MARY. What do I do?

CRICHTON. So—as if you were—*(he makes a movement)* washing them. I have noticed that the others tend to do it also.

LADY MARY (*archly*). Oh, Gov.—have you forgotten?

CRICHTON. Forgotten! What?

LADY MARY. That once on a time a certain other person did that!

CRICHTON (*surprised*). You mean myself? (LADY MARY *nods.*) How strange!

LADY MARY. You haven't for a very long time. Perhaps it is natural to servants. (*She turns towards the dresser.*)

CRICHTON. That must be it. (*He rises.*) Polly!

(LADY MARY *turns. He sighs heavily.*)

LADY MARY (*she takes off the wreath, and placing it on the dresser, crosses to below the table*). You sighed, Gov.

CRICHTON. Did I? (*He crosses to up* C.) I was thinking. (LADY MARY *crosses to below the chair* R.C. CRICHTON *then crosses to top of the table at the* R. *edge.*) I have always tried to do the right thing on this island. Above all, Polly, I want to do the right thing by you.

LADY MARY. How we all trust you! That is your reward, Gov.

CRICHTON (*moving towards her.*) Oh, Polly, I want a greater reward—— (*Taking her hand—much moved.*) Am I playing the game? Bill Crichton would like always to play the game. If we were in England—! (*He turns* L. *and goes to the table.*)

LADY MARY (*coming up* C., *above and on his* R.). We know now that we shall never see England again.

CRICHTON (R. *of the table, facing front*). I am thinking, Polly, of two people whom neither of us has seen for a long time—Lady Mary Lasenby, and one Crichton, a butler.

LADY MARY. That cold, haughty, indolent girl! Gov., look around you and forget them both.

CRICHTON *(moves to* C.*)*. I had nigh forgotten them, Polly. *(He sinks into the chair.)* He has had a chance—that butler—he's had a chance in these years of becoming a man, and he has tried to take it. There have been many failures, but there has been some success, and with it all I have let the past drop away, and turned my back on it. There's something so grand to me in feeling myself a man. That butler seems a far-away figure to me now, and not myself—I hail him, but we scarce know each other—if I am to bring him back it can only be done by force—for in my soul he is now abhorrent to me. *(Speaking more slowly.)* But if I thought it best for you—if I thought it best for you, I'd drag him back—I swear as an honest man I would bring him back to you with all his obsequious ways and deferential airs, and let you see the man you call your Gov. melt for ever into him who was your servant.

LADY MARY *(down to* L. *of* CRICHTON*)*. You hurt me. You say these things, but you say them—like a king.

CRICHTON *(rising)*. A king! A king! I sometimes feel-- *(He checks himself.)* I say it harshly, it is hard to say, and all the time there is another voice within me crying—

LADY MARY. If it is the voice of Nature—

CRICHTON. I know it is the voice of Nature.

LADY MARY. Then if you want to say it—very much, Gov.—please say it to Polly Lasenby.

CRICHTON. Polly, some people hold that the soul but leaves one human tenement for another, and so lives on through the ages. In some past existence I may have been a king—who knows? It has all come to me so naturally, not as if I had had to work it out, but as if I remembered. *(He quotes.)*

> "Or ever the knightly years were gone
>   With the old world to the grave
>   I was a *king* in Babylon,
>   And you were a Christian slave."

It may have been—you hear me, it may have been.

LADY MARY (*who is as one fascinated; backing a pace*). It may have been.

CRICHTON. I am lord over all—they are but hewers of wood and drawers of water for me—these shores are mine—why should I hesitate? I have no longer any doubt. I do believe *I am* doing the right thing. Polly, dear Polly. (*Crossing to her.*) Dear Polly, I have grown to love you—will you let John Treherne make us man and wife? (*He quotes again.*)

"I was a king in Babylon,
        And you were a Christian slave."

LADY MARY (*bewitched*). You are the most wonderful man I have ever known, and I am not afraid. (CRICHTON *takes her hand and kisses it with emotion—and reverently. There is a pause. He crosses and sits in the chair* R.C. *and motions her to sit on the ground in front of him. She does so.*) I want you to tell me—any woman likes to know—when was the first time you thought me nicer than the others?

CRICHTON. I think, a year ago. We were chasing goats on the Big Slope and you out-distanced us all, you were the first of our party to run a goat down—I was very proud of you that day.

LADY MARY. Gov.! I only did it to please you. Everything I have done has been out of the desire to please you. (*Suddenly.*) The others will be so jealous. (*Anxious.*) If I thought that in taking a wife from among us you were imperilling your dignity—

CRICHTON. Have no fear of that, dear. I have thought it all out. The wife, Polly, always takes the same position as the husband.

LADY MARY (*delighted*). Oh! (*Suddenly.*) I am so unworthy. It was sufficient to me that I should be allowed to wait on you at that table.

CRICHTON. You shall wait on me no longer. At whatever table I sit, Polly, you shall sit there also. (*He holds out a hand.*) Come, let us try what it will be like.

LADY MARY. At your feet?

CRICHTON. No, by my side.

(He conducts her to the table and motions her to sit in his chair at the top end. He sits below her and on her left, and they look delightedly at each other, stretching out and touching hands. LADY AGATHA has opened the serving-hatch to pass through a cup of coffee and is annoyed at what she sees. She taps for LADY MARY to come for the coffee. LADY MARY does not hear. LADY AGATHA taps again, and then signs to the others behind the hatch, and the three heads appear, watching indignantly. Then LADY CATHERINE opens the screen and comes in, switching on the "chandelier." This has no effect on the pair at the table. TWEENEY hands the tray to LADY AGATHA, who brings it down to L. of CRICHTON.)

CRICHTON *(not startled, but like one displeased with bad manners)*. Help your mistress first. *(The three women are speechless, but CRICHTON does not notice this. He addresses LADY CATHERINE vaguely as LADY AGATHA serves LADY MARY.)* Are you a good girl, Kitty?

(For a moment LADY CATHERINE cannot find her tongue. Then:)

LADY CATHERINE. I try to be, Gov.
CRICHTON. That's right.

(LADY CATHERINE is now L.C., above and R. of the table, with TWEENEY on her R., and LADY AGATHA has moved above them to stand R. of TWEENEY. ERNEST enters quickly down L., but on seeing CRICHTON, pauses and stands there meekly. CRICHTON rises and speaks graciously to them all.)

CRICHTON. Sit down! Sit down! *(He crosses up C. as LADY AGATHA sits on the seat R., TWEENEY up R.C. by the window, LADY CATHERINE on a stool R. of the table, and ERNEST on the stool below the dresser, which he pulls out, first transferring the concertina to the*

floor. Turning down above and to R. *of the table.)*
Ernest! (ERNEST *rises and stands—*CRICHTON *speaks firmly but good-naturedly.)* You are becoming a little slovenly in your dress, Ernest—I don't like it.

ERNEST *(respectfully).* Thank you. *(He sits.)*

*(*CRICHTON *resumes his walk up to the kitchen again. Enter at the door* L. LORD LOAM *and* TREHERNE R. *They look in surprise at the situation.)*

LORD LOAM *(crossing to the top of the table).* Why —what—?

*(*ERNEST *signs for silence.)*

CRICHTON *(going up* C.*).* Daddy, I want you. *(He crosses and looks into the fire again.)*

LORD LOAM *(alarmed, crossing up* R.C. *to* TWEENEY *and whispering to her).* Is it because I forgot to clean out the dam?

*(*CRICHTON *crosses down to above the table and pours out some wine in the goblet.)*

CRICHTON *(holding up the goblet).* Daddy, a glass of wine with you.

*(*LORD LOAM *moves* C. *in amazement and takes the goblet.)*

LORD LOAM *(takes goblet).* Your health, Gov. *(He is about to drink.)*

CRICHTON *(holds up goblet).* And hers! *(He moves a little up* C. LORD LOAM *looks to* TWEENY. *He drinks,* ALL *look surprised and the* GIRLS *disappointed.)* Daddy, this lady has done me the honour to promise to be my wife.

LORD LOAM *(astounded).* Polly?

CRICHTON *(puts the goblet down—moves towards*

LORD LOAM). I ought first to have asked your consent
—I deeply regret— But Nature—may I hope I have
your approval?

LORD LOAM. *May* you, Gov.! *(Delighted.) Rather!*
Polly! *(He crosses to behind and to her* L., *and em-
braces her.)*

(TWEENY *buries her face in her hands and cries
quietly.)*

TREHERNE *(crossing up to* C. *of* LADY MARY). We
all congratulate you, Gov., most heartily. *(He shakes
hands with* LADY MARY, *who rises and crosses to the
chair* R.C.)

ERNEST *(crossing to shake hands with* LADY MARY).
Long life to you both, sir. *(He crosses to the window,
sitting on the sill,* L. *of* TWEENY.)

(LORD LOAM *sits on the chair* LADY MARY *vacates.)*

LADY AGATHA. Dear Polly. *(Giving her cheek over
the back of the chair and then returns to the seat* R.)

(LADY AGATHA *and* LADY CATHERINE *affect to be delighted.* LADY CATHERINE *crosses, also gives her
cheek to* LADY MARY *and crosses back to* L.
CRICHTON *comes down to above* LADY MARY'S *chair*
C.)

TREHERNE *(up* L.C.). When will it be, Gov.?

CRICHTON *(questioning* LADY MARY, *crossing to
her).* As soon as the bridal skirt can be prepared. *(He
comes down* R. *of the chair with his back to the audience.)* My friends, I thank you for your good wishes.
I thank you all. *(He crosses up* C., L *of the chair and
turns.)* And now perhaps you would like me to leave
you to yourselves. Be joyous. Let there be song and
dance to-night, Daddy, I shall not complain of the
noise to-night. Polly, I shall take my coffee in the

parlour—you understand! *(He crosses to the passage up L.)* And remember, all of you, this lady is to be treated with as much deference as if she were already my wife—

(Exit CRICHTON *up* L. LADY MARY *rises, to* R. *of her chair.* LADY AGATHA *and* LADY CATHERINE *immediately rush at* LADY MARY *and pinch her. She backs up* R.C., LADY AGATHA *on her* R., LADY CATHERINE *on her* L. LORD LOAM *moves up* C.)

LADY MARY *(rises, backs up* C.). Oh, oh! Father, they are pinching me.

LORD LOAM *(pulling* LADY CATHERINE *away).* Catherine, Agatha, never presume to pinch your sister again. On the other hand she may pinch you henceforth as much as ever she chooses. *(He comes down* R. *of the table.)*

*(*TREHERNE *moves* L. *of the table.* LADY AGATHA *and* LADY CATHERINE *retire up stage.* LADY MARY *crosses in front of them to the table to get coffee, which she holds ostentatiously before her sisters and exits* L. *up stage, by the passage.* LORD LOAM *moves to the chair* C. *and is drinking his wine.* TWEENY *has slowly come down* R.C. *and sat on the seat* R. ERNEST *comes down to above the table* LC.)

LADY CATHERINE *(coming down* L. *of* TWEENY). Poor Tweeny, it's a shame.

LADY AGATHA *(coming down* R. *of* TWEENY, *and bending over her).* After he had almost promised *you.*

TWEENY. No, he never did. He was always honourable as could be. 'Twas me as was too vulgar. *(She rises.)* I tell you I'll crack your heads together if you say a word agint that man. Out of the way there.

*(*TWEENY *waves* LADY CATHERINE *aside and goes to the kitchen.* TREHERNE *goes up and comforts her.)*

ERNEST *(coming to behind* LORD LOAM, *draining* CRICHTON'S *goblet)*. You'll get a lot of tit-bits out of this, Daddy.

LORD LOAM. That's what I was thinking.

ERNEST *(turning up to the kitchen)*. I daresay *I* shall have to clean out the dam now.

LORD LOAM. I dare say. *(He jumps up and crosses to the table for the concertina, singing:)* "I'm a chicketty chicketty chick chick—" *(He picks up the concertina and hops across to* R., *continuing to sing.)*

*(*TREHERNE *comes down* C. LADY AGATHA *takes the back and* TREHERNE *the front of the armchair and they place it close to the window up* C.*)*

TREHERNE. That's the proper spirit! *(To down* R.C.*)* Kitty!

(He takes hold of her and during the next lines they dance to the music from C. *to* L. *and then to* R. *and back towards the* L. *door, just as* CRICHTON *enters.)*

ERNEST *(wanting to join)*. Tweeny?

TWEENY *(sitting on the stool by the fire)*. Not I.

ERNEST *(crossing to* LADY AGATHA*)*. Aggy—

(They dance with the other couple from R. *to* L. *and back to* R. *as* CRICHTON *enters with* LADY MARY. *At* CRICHTON'S *appearance* LORD LOAM *stops dead in his playing. Note.—*CRICHTON *has the feathered mantle on for this entrance—they turn away.)*

CRICHTON. No, no, I am delighted to see you all so happy. Go on, go on.

TREHERNE (R.). They don't like to before you, Gov.

CRICHTON. It is my wish. *(He moves to below the chair up* C.*)*

*(*TREHERNE *crosses to the table.* ERNEST, *at* L., *takes*

the bottom of the table, TREHERNE *the top, and they place it well* L. ERNEST *puts the stool* L. *back against the wall.* TREHERNE *puts the stools* L.C. *under the table.* LADY CATHERINE *moves the chair at the head of the table to* L., *and stands for* CRICHTON *to sit in it.* LADY MARY *asks* TWEENY *to join in and she consents. From the time* CRICHTON *says* "It is my wish" *until* ALL *are in their places,* LORD LOAM *gives one long chord on his concertina and is sitting on the seat* R., *down stage.* ALL (*except* CRICHTON *and* LORD LOAM) *go into a dance, of a country type. When the dancing is at its height the boom of a gun is heard, and all stop suddenly as if turned to stone.* ERNEST *runs to the window and stands on the sill looking out.*)

TREHERNE (L.C.). It was a ship's gun. (*He turns to* CRICHTON.) Gov.!

(ALL *look to* CRICHTON *for confirmation.*)

CRICHTON. Yes!

(*He goes up to the small window up* C. *and looks out.* ERNEST *jumps out of the long window followed by* TREHERNE *and* TWEENY. LADY AGATHA *holds out her hand to* LADY CATHERINE *and they exit* R. CRICHTON *looks at* LADY MARY, *who is* C., *then at* LORD LOAM. LORD LOAM *is sitting weakly.*)

LADY MARY (*turning to look out of the window, then crossing to* L. *of her father*). Father, you heard?
LORD LOAM (*placidly*). Yes, my child.
LADY MARY (*alarmed at his unnatural calm*). But it was a gun, Father!
LORD LOAM. Yes—a gun—I have often heard it. It's only a dream, you know—why don't we go on dancing?
LADY MARY (*comes down* C. *facing him—takes the*

concertina from him). Don't you see, they have all rushed down to the beach? Come!

(CRICHTON *moves to the long window up* R.C.)

LORD LOAM. Rushed down to the beach—yes, always that—I often dream it.

LADY MARY. Come, Father, come!

LORD LOAM. Only a dream, my poor girl.

(CRICHTON *comes down* C.)

CRICHTON (C.). We can see the lights within a mile from the shore—a great ship.

LORD LOAM *(quietly)*. A ship—always a ship.

LADY MARY *(comes behind him, she puts her hand on his shoulder and looks into his face)*. Father, this is no dream.

LORD LOAM *(rising and turning to* LADY MARY). It's a dream, isn't it? There's no ship? *(He turns to* CRICHTON.)

CRICHTON *(down* C., *kindly)*. You are awake, Daddy; there is a ship.

LORD LOAM *(crossing and clutching* CRICHTON). You are not—deceiving me?

CRICHTON. It is the truth.

LORD LOAM. True—a ship *(turning away* R.) —a ship—at last!

(He staggers out of the room R. *and goes after the* OTHERS. LADY MARY *gives way, and moves up* R.C.)

CRICHTON. (C.). There is a small boat between it and the island—they must have sent it ashore for water.

(LADY MARY *looks out of the window.)*

LADY MARY *(huskily)*. Coming in?

CRICHTON *(moving up to slightly* R. *of* C.). No—

that gun must have been a signal to recall it. It is going
back. They can't hear our cries.

LADY MARY. Going away! *(She crosses down* R.C., *to
below the seat.)* So near—so near—I think I'm glad.

CRICHTON *(affecting cheerfulness—crossing above
and* L. *of her).* Have no fear. I shall bring them back.

LADY MARY *(turning to face* CRICHTON). What are
you going to do?

CRICHTON *(taking a step towards her).* Fire the
beacons. *(He turns a pace up* C.)

LADY MARY *(moving up on his* R.). Stop! (CRICHTON
turns to her, at C. LADY MARY *moves a pace towards
him.)* Don't you see what it means?

CRICHTON *(bravely firm).* It means—it means that
our life on the island has come to a natural end. *(He
takes a pace towards the switch.)*

LADY MARY *(stopping him—looking around).* Let
the ship go!

CRICHTON *(looking at* LADY MARY *for a moment).*
The old man—you saw what it means to him—

LADY MARY. But I was afraid!

CRICHTON *(adoringly, kissing her hand).* Ah, dear
Polly! *(He turns again towards the switch.)*

LADY MARY *(catches his arm).* No! *(Very kindly
but firmly he loosens her hold of him.)*

CRICHTON. Bill Crichton has got to play the game.

(He goes up and turns the lever. She turns up R., *below
the long window and looks out. There is a pause.
Then the light of the beacon begins to be seen, the
sky is slowly suffused with the glow of it. Then
another gun is heard and faint distant cheering and
shouts. This is all slowly done and during that time
CRICHTON and LADY MARY stand, very still, staring
out of the window to R. He is behind and several
paces from her. Presently the sky is very bright from
the beacon. LADY MARY turns, without looking at
CRICHTON, crosses slowly down L. and sits in the
chair set R. of the table against the L. wall. CRICHTON*

*then goes up into the kitchen and stares down into
the fire.* ERNEST *runs on excitedly outside the window, jumps over the ledge calling* "Polly!"—*he sees*
LADY MARY *and goes down to her.)*

ERNEST. Polly! The boat has turned back! We're
rescued! *(Above and on her* R.*)* I tell you—rescued!

LADY MARY. Is it anything to make so great a to-do
about?

ERNEST *(down a pace)*. Eh?

LADY MARY *(rising, and turning to him)*. Have we
not been happy here?

ERNEST *(crosses and takes spears from the wall)*.
Happy— Lord, yes!

LADY MARY *(imploringly)*. Ernest, we must never
forget all that the Gov. has done for us.

ERNEST *(stoutly)*. Forget it! The man who could
forget it would be a selfish wretch and a— *(A sudden
thought.)* But I say—this makes a difference.

LADY MARY *(quickly, her hand on his left arm)*. No,
it doesn't.

ERNEST *(Thinking of it)*. A mighty difference!

LADY MARY *(turning up to the passage up* L.*)*. Oh—
you— *(She exits.)*

(ERNEST *stares after her, then turns towards the windows. In the meantime the light has grown brighter
—the cheering is now nearer.* TWEENY *enters* R.
excitedly.)

TWEENY *(crosses to* R. *of* ERNEST *at* C.*)*. Ernest,
they've landed—they're English sailors—we're saved!
(She runs down L., *and exits.)*

ERNEST *(staring out of the windows)*. Saved! Saved!

(He turns quickly and exits down L. CRICHTON *has not
moved from the fireplace in the kitchen. Now he
turns to face down* R. *as* LADY AGATHA *rushes on,
crosses to the* L. *door, calls* LADY MARY, *runs up to
the door at the back, calls again, leans on the chair*
L.C. *and cries.* LADY CATHERINE *rushes in up* R.C. *at*

the window and cries for joy—TREHERNE, *following, comforts her.* LORD LOAM *enters* R., *followed by an* OFFICER, *and crosses a little* L. *of* C. CRICHTON *quietly comes down and stands up by the window up* C. *Two* SAILORS *stand outside the windows with lanterns and look in curiously.)*

(WARN Curtain.)

LORD LOAM *(to the* OFFICER, C.). And here, sir, in our little home itself, let me thank you in the name of us all, again and again and again.

OFFICER. Very proud, my lord! It is indeed an honour to have been able to assist so distinguished a gentleman as Lord Loam.

LORD LOAM. A glorious, glorious day! Let me show you our other rooms. *(He crosses to down* L.) Come, my pets— *(A pause: then turning at the door down* L.) Come, Crichton.

(LADY AGATHA, LADY CATHERINE, TREHERNE *and the* OFFICER *exit* L., *down stage. The* SAILORS *go from the window off* R. CRICHTON *moves slowly down stage* R. *of* C. LADY MARY *comes in softly* L., *up stage, and stretches out her arms.)*

LADY MARY *(crosses down a little,* L. *of* CRICHTON). Dear Gov.! I shall never give you up. (CRICHTON *slowly lets the cloak drop off him to the ground, staring out front.)* Gov.!

(She is vanquished—she withdraws slowly backwards to L. *up stage and stands gazing at him. He continues looking straight before him, fighting himself. At first he is a strong erect figure, but gradually he gets into the humbler bearing of a servant, his hands meet and rub together as they had done in Act I.)*

CRICHTON *(beginning to turn slowly towards her).* My lady! *(He is the butler again.)*

CURTAIN

ACT IV

SCENE.—*The same as Act I. Early summer evening.*

The furniture remains the same (except for changes of postion shown in the Furniture Plot), but there are one or two additions. A large glass case is set L., *between the windows, which is filled with curios from the island, including the bucket, suitably labelled.*

Other curios, also labelled, are in the china cabinet up C. *There are stuffed birds, animals' heads, weapons, and other trophies, with notices showing who destroyed the former, or used the latter.*

On the R. *settee, towards the* L. *end, sits* LORD LOAM. *He is searching the pages of a new book with much gilt on the covers. At his right side is the concertina.* LADY AGATHA *sits on the stool below the table* L. *of the settee, and* LADY CATHERINE *on the stool above it. They are in afternoon dress and have newspapers.* ERNEST *is sitting* L. *of the table, near them, looking very complacent. The manner of* ALL *of them is that of people apprehensive of the door opening and* CRICHTON *walking in.*

When the Curtain has risen, and the above state of mind has been registered, LADY AGATHA, *after a glance towards the doors up* L.C., *turns to face down stage again and reads from her paper.*

LADY AGATHA *(looks toward door* L.—*reading aloud facing the audience).* "In conclusion, we most heartily congratulate the Hon. Ernest Woolley. This book of his regarding the adventures of himself and his brave companions on a desert isle, stirs the heart like a trumpet." *(She puts down her paper and looks round to see what effect it has on the* OTHERS.)

ERNEST *(looks round at the door* L., *then takes the paper from beneath his waistcoat).* Here is another. *(He gives it to her.)*

LADY CATHERINE *(reading from her newspaper).* "From the first to the last of Mr. Woolley's engrossing pages it is evident that he was an ideal man to be wrecked with, and a true hero." *(Reprovingly.)* Ernest!

ERNEST. That's how it strikes them, you know. *(Looking round as before.)* Here's another one. *(He gives her another paper from beneath his waistcoat.)*

LADY AGATHA *(reading from her second newspaper).* "There is not much reference to the two servants who were wrecked with the family, but Mr. Woolley pays them a kindly tribute in a footnote." *(She looks at* ERNEST, *then looks at the door.)*

LORD LOAM. Excellent, excellent. At the same time, I must say, Ernest, that the whole book is about yourself.

ERNEST *(high-handed). As* the author—

LORD LOAM. Certainly, certainly. Still, you know, as a peer of the realm—*(with dignity)*—I think, Ernest, you might have given *me* one of the adventures.

ERNEST. I say it was you who taught us how to get a light by rubbing two pieces of stick together.

LORD LOAM *(beaming—eagerly).* Do you—do you? I call that handsome. What page? *(He searches eagerly in the book.)*

(Enter CRICHTON *quietly at up* L.C., *carrying three evening newspapers.* LADY AGATHA *throws her paper under the table and crosses to* R., *looking up.* LADY CATHERINE *throws her paper under the table and crosses to behind the settee* R. LORD LOAM *hides his book.* ERNEST *conceals another paper he is just drawing out from beneath his waistcoat.* CRICHTON *puts the evening papers on the table* R.C.)

LORD LOAM *(at last, as if someone had spoken).* Quite so—quite so.

(Exit CRICHTON *up* L.C. *There is a sigh of relief and each advances to the table rapidly and picks up a newspaper.)*

LADY CATHERINE. Father, the evening papers!

*(*ALL *look for the book reviews, and read.* ERNEST *smiles to himself over what he read, then evidently reads something unpleasant, and dashes the paper to the ground.)*

LADY AGATHA *(again seated below the table* R.C.*).* Father, see page eighty-one! *(*LORD LOAM *tries to find the page.* LADY AGATHA *reads.)* "It was a tiger cat," says Mr. Woolley, "of the largest size. Death stared Lord Loam in the face, but he never flinched."

LORD LOAM *(searching frantically).* Page—eighty—one—

LADY AGATHA. "With presence of mind only equalled by his courage, he fixed an arrow in his bow—"

LORD LOAM. Thank you, Ernest; thank you, my boy.

LADY AGATHA. "Unfortunately he missed—"

LORD LOAM. Eh?

LADY AGATHA. "But by good luck I heard his cries—"

LORD LOAM. My cries!

LADY AGATHA. "And rushing forward with drawn knife I stabbed the monster to the heart."

(A pause. ERNEST *folds his arms.* LORD LOAM *throws his book on the floor. Enter* CRICHTON *quietly up* R.C.; *crosses to the cabinet up* L. *and opens it. They* ALL *hide their papers.)*

LORD LOAM. Anything in the papers, Catherine?

LADY CATHERINE. No, Father; nothing—nothing at all.

*(*CRICHTON, *up* L., *takes the bucket from the cabinet and puts it on the floor and closes the cabinet.)*

ERNEST. The papers! The papers are guides that tell us what we ought to do and then we don't do it. Ha! Ha!

(CRICHTON *is crossing up stage from* L. *to* R., *not looking at them, and carrying the bucket in his* L. *hand as* ERNEST *looks round for approval and sees the bucket. He rises fearfully and follows* CRICHTON *to the door up* R.C., *quite resigned to get a dipping when the door closes in his face. He staggers back to* C., *realizing his mistake.*)

LORD LOAM *(looking across* C. *at* ERNEST). I told him to take it away.

ERNEST *(standing* C.). I thought— *(He wipes his brow with a handkerchief.)* I shall go and dress.

(He exits up L.C. *with a swagger. The* OTHERS *are uncomfortable.)*

LADY CATHERINE *(nervously—crosses to behind the settee* R. *of* LORD LOAM). Father, it's awful having Crichton here! It's like living on tiptoe.

LORD LOAM. While he is here we are sitting on a volcano.

LADY AGATHA. But he is too splendid to divulge anything unless—unless people got suspicious and questioned him. Crichton's one failing is that he simply can't tell a fib.

LADY CATHERINE *(moving down* R. *of the settee).* Suppose Lady Brocklehurst were to get at him and pump him! She's the most terrifying old creature in England.

LADY AGATHA *(rising and going down* L.C.). Don't suppose anything so awful. *(She moves up toward the table* L.C.)

LORD LOAM *(tragically).* My dear, that is the volcano to which I was referring. (LADY AGATHA *turns sharply.* LADY CATHERINE *comes in a pace* R.C. *and* BOTH stare at LORD LOAM.) It's all Mary's fault. She said to me yesterday that she would break her engagement with Brocklehurst unless I told him about—you know what. *(He looks at the door up R.C.)*

LADY AGATHA *(moving to R. of the armchair L.C.)* Is she mad?

LORD LOAM. She calls it common honesty.

(LADY AGATHA turns away impatiently down L. and sits on the L. settee.)

LADY CATHERINE *(facing him)*. Father, have you told him? *(She sits in the chair down R.)*

LORD LOAM. She thinks I have, but—I couldn't. She's sure to find out to-night. *(He puts his hand unconsciously on the concertina—it squeaks—they ALL jump up.)*

LADY AGATHA. Oh!

LADY CATHERINE. It's like a bird of ill omen.

LORD LOAM. I must have it taken away; it's done that twice.

(LADY AGATHA goes up above the table L.C., fanning herself. LADY CATHERINE and LORD LOAM sit again. Enter LADY MARY up L.C. in evening dress. She enters swaggering in manly fashion—then sees that she has done so and adopts an anxiously ladylike manner.)

LADY MARY *(C.)*. Agatha! *(She looks round—signs that she wants to be left alone with LORD LOAM and moves down L.C.)*

LADY AGATHA *(crossing to up C.)*. All right, but we know what it's about. *(She looks at LADY CATHERINE.)* Come along, Kit.

(LADY CATHERINE moves up C., turning here and looking at LADY MARY anxiously. Then both GIRLS exit up L.C. LADY MARY crosses and sits R.C. on the chair

below the table R.C., *crossing the right leg like a boy. She notices this and hurriedly uncrosses it.* LORD LOAM *has not looked up.)*

LADY MARY *(with her back half turned to* LORD LOAM*).* Father! *(He doesn't look up.)* Father! *(She whistles sharply to attract him—he starts—so does she —she is in despair.)* How horrid of me.

LORD LOAM. If you could try to remember.

LADY MARY. I do, but— *(Sadly.)* There are so many things to remember.

LORD LOAM *(sympathetically).* There are! *(Nervously.)* Do you know, Mary, I constantly find myself secreting hairpins.

LADY MARY. I find it so difficult to go up steps one at a time.

LORD LOAM *(staring out front).* I was dining with half a dozen Cabinet Ministers last Thursday, Mary, and I couldn't help wondering all the time how many of them he would have set to cleaning the dam.

LADY MARY. I use so many of his phrases. And my appetite is so scandalous. Father— (LORD LOAM *looks at her.)* I usually have a chop before we sit down to dinner.

LORD LOAM *(nods sympathetically).* As for my clothes, *(wriggling at his collar)* my dear, you can't think how irksome collars are to me nowadays.

LADY MARY. They can't be half such an annoyance, Father, as— *(Holding up her skirt.)*

LORD LOAM. Quite so—quite so. You have dressed early, Mary.

LADY MARY *(turns to him).* That reminds me—I had a note from Brocklehurst saying that he would come a few minutes before his mother as—as he wanted to have a talk with me. (LORD LOAM *rises and moves away* R. *to the fireplace.)* He didn't say what about, but of course we know.

LORD LOAM *(turning and crossing to* C.*).* I—ah— *(He passes her, nervously.)*

LADY MARY *(finding it difficult to say—stretches out her hands and catches his arm)*. It was good of you to tell him, Father. Oh, it is horrible to me *(covering her face)*—it seemed so *natural* at the time. *(She turns down R.C.)*

LORD LOAM *(petulantly—coming behind* LADY MARY *and hitting the table)*. Never again make use of that word in this house, Mary. *(He sits on the chair L. of the table.)*

LADY MARY *(turning at R.C.)*. Father. Brocklehurst has been so loyal to me for these two years that I should despise myself were I to keep my—my extraordinary lapse from him. Had Brocklehurst been only a little less good—then you need not have told him—my—strange little secret.

LORD LOAM. Polly—I mean Mary—it was all Crichton's fault, he—

LADY MARY *(crossing him to C.)*. No, Father, no—not a word against him. *(She turns at C.)* I haven't the pluck to go on with it—I can't even understand how it ever was *(moving above the chair R.C.)*—Father, do you not still hear the surf? Do you see the curve of the beach?

LORD LOAM *(staring out front)*. I have begun to forget. But they were happy days—there was something magical about them.

LADY MARY. It was glamour. Father, I have lived Arabian nights. I have sat out a dance with the evening star. *(She sits on the stool above the table R.C.)* But it was all in a past existence, in the days of Babylon, and I am myself again. But he has been chivalrous always. If the slothful, indolent creature I used to be has improved in any way I owe it all to him. I am slipping back in many ways, but I am determined not to slip, back altogether—in memory of *him* and *his* island. *(She rises.)* That is why I insisted on your telling Brocklehurst. *(Crossing down* L.C.*)* He can break our engagement if he chooses.

LORD LOAM. But, my dear—

(Enter CRICHTON up L.C. and stands below and R. of the doors.)

CRICHTON. Lord Brocklehurst.

(LORD BROCKLEHURST enters, crosses C. and shakes hands with LORD LOAM. He then crosses and shakes hands with LADY MARY at L.C. CRICHTON, during this exits up L.C., closing the doors.)

LADY MARY. Father, dear, oughtn't you to be dressing?

LORD LOAM (R. *of* LORD BROCKLEHURST). The fact is—before I go—I want to say—

LORD BROCKLEHURST *(turning to* LORD LOAM). Loam, if you don't mind, I wish very specially to have a word with Mary before dinner.

LORD LOAM. But—

LADY MARY. Yes, Father. (LORD LOAM *crosses up* R., *and exits, uneasily.* LORD BROCKLEHURST *moves to* R. *of* C., *watching him off. He is grave and awkward.* LADY MARY, *strained and nervous, turns to below the table* L.C. LORD BROCKLEHURST *picks up a paper nervously.)* I am ready, George.

LORD BROCKLEHURST *(putting down the paper).* It is a painful matter—I wish I could have spared you this, Mary. *(He is agitated.)*

LADY MARY. Please go on. *(She sits on the stool* L.C.)

LORD BROCKLEHURST *(moving to* C.). In common fairness, of course, this should be remembered—that two years had elapsed. You and I had no reason to believe that we should ever meet again.

LADY MARY *(gazing down, towards* L.C.). I was so lost to the world, George.

LORD BROCKLEHURST *(firmly).* At the same time the thing is utterly and absolutely inexcusable.

LADY MARY *(drawing herself up).* Oh!

LORD BROCKLEHURST. And so I have already said to Mother.

LADY MARY *(freezing).* You have told *her!*

LORD BROCKLEHURST *(moving a pace towards her).* Certainly, Mary, certainly, I tell Mother everything.

LADY MARY. And what *did* she say?

LORD BROCKLEHURST *(looking down R.C.).* To tell the truth, Mother pooh-poohed the whole affair.

LADY MARY *(amazed—rising).* Lady Brocklehurst pooh-poohed the whole affair?

LORD BROCKLEHURST. She said, "Mary and I will have a good laugh over this."

LADY MARY *(furious).* George! *(Crossing him to R.C. and turning.)* Your mother is a hateful, depraved old woman!

LORD BROCKLEHURST *(much shocked).* Mary!

LADY MARY. Laugh indeed! *(She sits on the stool R.C.)* When it will always be such a pain to me.

LORD BROCKLEHURST *(crosses to her L.).* If only you would let me bear all the pain, Mary.

LADY MARY *(astounded).* George, I think you are the noblest man— *(She gives him her left hand, which he takes.)*

LORD BROCKLEHURST *(caressing her hand and looking away).* She was a pretty little thing. (LADY MARY *looks up in astonishment. He releases her hand.)* Ah, not beautiful like you. (LADY MARY *stares. He drops down a pace or two L.C., and turns.)* I assure you it was the merest flirtation—there *were* a few letters, but we have got them back. It was all owing to the boat being so late at Calais—you see, she had such large, helpless eyes. *(He moves to down L.C.)*

(After a slight pause.)

LADY MARY *(controlling her feelings).* George, when you lunched with Father to-day at the club—

LORD BROCKLEHURST *(moving up R. of the armchair L.C.).* I didn't. He wired me that he couldn't come.

LADY MARY. But he wrote you?

LORD BROCKLEHURST. No.

LADY MARY. You haven't seen him since?

LORD BROCKLEHURST. No.

LADY MARY. Then— *(She rises delighted as she realizes he knows nothing—then suddenly becoming terrible—turns to him.)* George, who and what is this woman?

LORD BROCKLEHURST *(coming towards her C.,—ashamed).* She was—she is— Oh, the shame of it! A lady's maid.

LADY MARY (R.C.). A what?

LORD BROCKLEHURST *(looking away L.).* A lady's maid. (LADY MARY *waves her handkerchief delightedly, unseen by him—moving down* R.C. *a little.)* I first met her at this house when you were entertaining the servants, so you see it was largely your father's fault.

LADY MARY. A lady's maid—

LORD BROCKLEHURST. Her name was Fisher.

LADY MARY. My maid!

LORD BROCKLEHURST *(taking a pace towards her).* Can you forgive me, Mary?

LADY MARY *(moving to him).* Oh, George, George!

LORD BROCKLEHURST. Mother urged me not to tell you anything about it, but—

LADY MARY. I am so glad you told me.

LORD BROCKLEHURST. You see, there was nothing wrong in it.

LADY MARY *(sitting below the table* R.C.). No, indeed. *(She is thinking of her own affair.)*

LORD BROCKLEHURST *(coming near her).* And she behaved awfully well. She quite saw that it was because the boat was late. I suppose the glamour to a girl in service of a man in high position—

LADY MARY *(staring out front).* Glamour—yes, yes, *that* was it!

LORD BROCKLEHURST. Mother says that a girl in such circumstances is to be excused if she loses her head.

LADY MARY. George, I am so sorry if I said anything against your mother. I am sure she is the dearest old thing.

LORD BROCKLEHURST (*moving to* C., *and turning there*). Of course for women of *our* class she has a very different standard.

LADY MARY (*feebly*). Of course. (*She looks away.*)

LORD BROCKLEHURST (*moving a little down* L.C.). You see, knowing how good a woman she is herself, she was naturally anxious that I should marry someone like her. That is what has always made her watch your conduct so jealously, Mary.

LADY MARY I know. (*Rising.*) I—I think, George, that before your mother comes I should like to say a word to Father.

LORD BROCKLEHURST (*nervously*). About—this?

LADY MARY. Oh, no—I shan't tell him of this. About something else.

LORD BROCKLEHURST (*coming to* C.). And you do forgive me, Mary?

LADY MARY (*moving towards him*). Yes—yes— (*Taking his hand.*) I—I am sure the boat was *very* late, George.

LORD BROCKLEHURST. It really was. (*Putting an arm round* LADY MARY'S *waist.*)

LADY MARY. I am even relieved to know that you are not quite perfect, dear. (*She crosses him to* C., *and then turns.*) George, when we are married we shall try to be not an entirely frivolous couple, won't we? We must try to be of some little use, dear.

LORD BROCKLEHURST. *Noblesse oblige.*

LADY MARY. Yes, yes, I am determined not to be a shirker, George. (LORD BROCKLEHURST *looks at her. She turns away as if she feels she is not quite playing the game.*) Except just this once. (*She crosses above the chair* R.C., *and turns—holding out her hand.*) George! (LORD BROCKLEHURST *crosses to her and kisses her. She disengages, moves up to the door up* R.C., *and turns there.*) I am so glad she was only a lady's maid.

(*She exits up* R.C., *leaving him happy and relieved. He moves down* R.C. *Enter* CRICHTON L.C.)

CRICHTON. The Countess of Brocklehurst.

(LADY BROCKLEHURST enters. She is a very formidable old lady who has also a sense of humour. CRICHTON switches on some lights and exits up R.C.)

LADY BROCKLEHURST *(looking around, seeing no one.* L.C.*).* Alone, George?

LORD BROCKLEHURST *(crosses to* R. *of* LADY BROCKLEHURST*).* Mother, I told her all. She has behaved magnificently.

LADY BROCKLEHURST. Silly boy! *(She turns up to the glass case* L.*)* So these are the wonders they brought back with them. *(She takes one up.)* Gone away to dry her eyes, I suppose?

LORD BROCKLEHURST *(proudly).* She didn't cry, Mother.

LADY BROCKLEHURST. No? *(She reflects.)* You're quite right—I wouldn't have cried. Cold, icy. Yes, that was it. *(At the cabinet, looking at a curio. She brings the curio across to above the table* L.C.*)*

LORD BROCKLEHURST *(moving towards her).* I assure you, Mother, that wasn't it at all. She forgave me at once.

LADY BROCKLEHURST *(sharply).* Oh! *(She puts down the curio.)*

LORD BROCKLEHURST. She was awfully nice about the boat being late—she even said she was relieved to find that I wasn't quite perfect.

LADY BROCKLEHURST *(sharply).* She said that?

LORD BROCKLEHURST. She really did. *(He crosses down* L.C.*)*

LADY BROCKLEHURST. I mean I wouldn't. *(She moves thoughtfully to* C.*)* Now if *I* had said that, what would have made me say it? *(She reflects—her suspicions growing.)* George, is Mary all we think her?

LORD BROCKLEHURST *(looking at her).* If she wasn't, Mother, you would know it!

LADY BROCKLEHURST. Hold your tongue. We don't really know what happened on that island.

LORD BROCKLEHURST *(taking a pace or two to* C.*).* You were reading the book all the morning.

LADY BROCKLEHURST. How can I be sure that the book is true!

LORD BROCKLEHURST. They all talk of it as true.

LADY BROCKLEHURST. How do I know that they are not lying?

LORD BROCKLEHURST. Why should they?

LADY BROCKLEHURST. Why shouldn't they? *(She crosses to* R.*, below the settee.)* If I had been wrecked on an island— *(She reflects.)* I think it is highly probable that *I* should have lied when I came back. *(She turns to him.)* Weren't their servants with them?

LORD BROCKLEHURST. Crichton, the butler. (LADY BROCKLEHURST *crosses to* R. *to the fireplace, pauses, rings the bell and moves to the table* R.*)* Why, Mother, you are not going to—

LADY BROCKLEHURST. Yes, I am— (R. *of the table, facing him, speaking very pointedly.)* George, watch whether Crichton begins any of his answers to my questions with "The fact is," because that is always the beginning of a lie. *(She sits on the settee* R. LORD BROCKLEHURST *crosses* R. *and stands with his back to the fireplace. Enter* CRICHTON *up* L.C. *He looks to see who rang—sees* LADY BROCKLEHURST.*)* It was I who rang. (CRICHTON *crosses to* L. *of the table* R.*)* So you were one of the castaways, Crichton?

CRICHTON. Yes, my lady.

LADY BROCKLEHURST. Delightful book Mr. Woolley has written about your adventures. *(She speaks sharply.)* Don't you think so?

CRICHTON. I have not read it, my lady.

LADY BROCKLEHURST. Odd they should not have presented *you* with a copy.

LORD BROCKLEHURST *(coming to* R. *of* LADY BROCKLEHURST*).* The book was only published to-day, Mother.

LADY BROCKLEHURST *(waving him away)*. Sh! *(To* CRICHTON.) I think you were not the only servant wrecked?

CRICHTON. There was a young woman, my lady.

LADY BROCKLEHURST. I want to see her. (CRICHTON *bows, but remains.)* Fetch her up.

(Exit CRICHTON *up* R.C.)

LORD BROCKLEHURST. This is scandalous!

LADY BROCKLEHURST. I am a mother— *(Enter* LADY CATHERINE *and* LADY AGATHA *in evening dress up* L.C. *They are terrified at the sight of* LADY BROCKLE- HURST, *but move down* C. *Shaking hands.)* How d'you do, Agatha?

*(*LADY AGATHA *moves away to* L.C.)*

LADY CATHHERINE *(*L. *of the table).* How do you do, Lady Brocklehurst?

(She shakes hands and turns to R. *of* LADY AGATHA. *They stand together, nervously.)*

LADY BROCKLEHURST *(regarding them)*. You didn't dress like this on the island, I expect. By the way, how *did* you dress?

*(*LADY AGATHA *and* LADY CATHERINE *clutch each other.)*

LADY AGATHA *(anxiously)*. Not—not so well, of course, but quite the same idea.

(Enter CRICHTON.)

CRICHTON. Mr. Treherne.

(Enter TREHERNE. CRICHTON *withdraws.* LADY CATH- ERINE, *relieved, turns up to meet* TREHERNE *who is*

in clerical dress. She intimates that LADY BROCKLE-
HURST *is there. He crosses and shakes hands with*
LADY BROCKLHURST, *above the table.)*

LADY BROCKLEHURST. How d'you do, Mr. Treherne?
There is not so much of you in the book as I had hoped.
    TREHERNE *(modestly).* There wasn't very much of
me on the island, Lady Brocklehurst. *(The* GIRLS, *hover-
ing at* L.C., *are on needles.)* Only that I did my best; it
was a rather poor best.
    LADY BROCKLEHURST. I thought that cricket educated
Englishmen for everything.
    TREHERNE. I used to think so, too. *(He crosses down
L. of the settee to R., and shakes hands with* LORD
BROCKLEHURST.)
    LORD BROCKLEHURST *(to* TREHERNE*).* I hear you've
got a living. Congratulations.
    TREHERNE. Thanks.
    LORD BROCKLHURST. Is it a good one?
    TREHERNE. So-so! They are rather weak in bowling,
but it's a good bit of turf.

(He crosses up R. *and meets* ERNEST *who enters up*
R.C.*)*

ERNEST *(crosses* C. *and shakes hands with* LADY
BROCKLEHURST *across the back of the settee).* How do
you do, Lady Brocklehurst?

*(*LADY CATHERINE *joins* TREHERNE *up* R.C.*)*

LADY BROCKLEHURST. Our brilliant author. It is
as engrossing, Mr. Woolley, as if it were a work of
fiction.
    ERNEST *(doubtful of her).* Thanks awfully. The fact
is—

(He stops, puzzled because LORD BROCKLEHURST *and*
LADY BROCKLEHURST *exchange significant glances,*

and withdraws a little towards C. LADY CATHERINE
takes TREHERNE *by the arm and brings him down to
above the settee.* ERNEST *moves down* L. *of the chair*
R.C.)

LADY CATHERINE. Lady Brocklehurst, Mr. Treherne
and I—we are engaged.

LADY AGATHA (*moving* C. *to* ERNEST). And Ernest
and I—

LADY BROCKLEHURST. I see, my dears—thought it
was wise to keep the island in the family.

(LADY AGATHA *and* ERNEST *move down* L.C. ALL *are
perturbed.* LADY CATHERINE *and* TREHERNE *break
a little* R. *as enter* LORD LOAM *and* LADY MARY *up*
L.C., *happy and gay. They come down.*)

LORD LOAM (*crossing to behind the settee* R., *and
looking down at* LADY BROCKLEHURST). Aha! Ha! ha!—
younger than any of them, Emily.

LADY BROCKLEHURST. Flatterer! (*To* LADY MARY,
who runs to her and sits on her L.) You seem in high
spirits, Mary.

LADY MARY. I am.

LADY BROCKLEHURST. After—? (*With a significant
glance at* LORD BROCKLEHURST.)

LADY MARY. I—I mean I—the fact is— (*She stops,
seeing* LORD BROCKLEHURST *is startled.*)

LORD LOAM (*gaily*). She hears wedding bells, Emily.

LADY BROCKLEHURST (*coolly*). Do you, Mary? Can't
say I do, but I'm hard of hearing.

LADY MARY (*rising haughtily*). If you don't, Lady
Brocklehurst, I'm sure I don't. (*She moves to below the
chair* L. *of the settee and turns up.*)

LORD LOAM. Tut, tut. (*He moves, nervously, over to
C.*) Seen our curios from the island, Emily? I should
like you to examine them.

LADY BROCKLEHURST. Thank you, Henry, I am glad
you say that, for I have just taken the liberty of asking
two of them to step upstairs.

(ALL *register consternation by exchanging glances.*
LADY MARY *gives her father a quick look.* LORD LOAM
crosses to above the armchair R.C. LADY MARY *turns
away to the top of the table* L.C. *Enter* CRICHTON *with*
TWEENY *in neat maid's dress—she is timid. They
stand up* C.)

LORD BROCKLEHURST *(stoutly)*. Loam, I have *no*
hand in this.

(LADY AGATHA *crosses down in front of the settee* L.
and sits.)

LADY BROCKLEHURST. Pooh, what have I done? You
always begged me to speak to the servants, Henry, and
I merely wanted to discover whether the views you
used to hold about equality were adopted on the island—
it seemed a splendid opportunity, but Mr. Woolley
has not a word on the subject.

(ALL *appeal to* ERNEST.)

ERNEST *(crossing to* L.C.). The fact is— *(He backs
to* R. *of* LADY AGATHA, *seeing* LORD BROCKLEHURST
and LADY BROCKLEHURST *exchange glances.)*
LORD LOAM *(moving towards* LADY BROCKLEHURST).
I assure you, Emily—
LADY MARY *(boldly—crossing and putting her hand
on* LORD LOAM's *arm)*. Father, nothing whatever happened on the island of which I, for one, am ashamed,
and I hope Crichton will be allowed to answer Lady
Brocklehurst's questions.
LADY BROCKLEHURST. To be sure. (LADY MARY,
after a cold glance at LADY BROCKLEHURST, *returns to
up* L.C.) There's nothing to make a fuss about and
we're a family party. (LORD LOAM *sits in the chair* L.
of the settee R.) Now— *(She beckons.* CRICHTON *comes
down* C.) Truthfully, my man.
CRICHTON. I promise that, my lady.

LADY BROCKLEHURST *(sharply)*. Well, were you all equal on the island?

CRICHTON. No, my lady—I think I may say there was as little equality there as elsewhere.

LADY BROCKLEHURST. All the social distinctions were preserved?

CRICHTON. As at home, my lady.

LADY BROCKLEHURST. The servants?

CRICHTON. They had to keep their place.

LADY BROCKLEHURST. Wonderful! How was it managed? *(Suddenly beckoning to* TWEENY, *who now comes down* L. *of* CRICHTON.*)* You, girl, tell me that. *(There is general anxiety as* TWEENY *is seen to hesitate. Only. * CRICHTON *is quite impassive.)* Come!

TWEENY. It was all the Gov.'s doing, your ladyship.

*(*ERNEST *sits beside* LADY AGATHA *on the settee* L. *There is a pause in which they all give themselves up for lost.)*

CRICHTON. In the regrettable slang of the servants' hall, my lady, the master is usually referred to as the Gov.

LADY BROCKLEHURST. I see—you— *(Looking at* LORD LOAM.*)*

LORD LOAM. Yes, I understand that is what they call me.

(There is general relief.)

LADY BROCKLEHURST. You didn't even take your meals with the family?

CRICHTON. No, my lady. I dined apart.

LADY BROCKLEHURST. You also— *(To* TWEENY, *who is scared.)* Come, did you dine with Crichton?

TWEENY *(terrified)*. No, your ladyship.

LADY BROCKLEHURST *(triumphant)*. With whom?

TWEENY. I took my bit of supper with—with Daddy and Polly and—the rest.

*(A suppressed display of awful discomfort—*Lady Brocklehurst *looks at* Tweeny *inquiringly.)*

Ernest *(brightly)*. Dear old Daddy—he was our monkey—you remember our monkey, Agatha?

Lady Agatha. Rather! What a funny darling he was!

Lady Catherine *(coming to above settee* R.*)*. And don't you think Polly was the sweetest little parrot, Mary?

Lady Brocklehurst. Ah! I understand—animals you had domesticated?

Lord Loam. Quite so—quite so. *(He is immensely relieved.)*

Lady Brocklehurst. The servants' teas that used to take place here once a month—

Crichton. They didn't seem natural on an island, my lady, and were discontinued—by the Gov.'s orders.

Lord Brocklehurst. A clear proof, Loam, that they were a mistake here.

Lord Loam *(rises)*. I admit it frankly—I abandon them, Emily, as the result of our experiences on the island. I think of going over to the Tories.

Lady Brocklehurst. I am delighted to hear it.

Lord Loam *(crossing up* R.C.*)*. Thank you, Crichton, thank you—that is all.

(He motions to Crichton *and* Tweeny, *who turn and go up stage.* Lady Mary *crosses down* L. *of the table* L.C.*)*

Lady Brocklehurst. One moment. *(*Crichton *checks and turns to face her.)* One moment, Crichton. *(*Crichton *comes down* C. Lady Mary *sits in the chair* L.C.*)* Young people, Crichton, will be young people even on an island—perhaps especially on an island—now, I suppose there was a certain amount of—shall we say sentimentalizing going on?

Crichton. Yes, my lady, there was.

LORD BROCKLEHURST (*angry*). Mother!

LADY BROCKLEHURST. Which gentleman? (*To* TWEENY). You, girl, tell me.

TWEENY (*comes down*). If you please, my lady—

ERNEST (*rises and moves forward—quickly*). The fact is— (*He is stopped as before, by glances.*)

TWEENY (*suddenly*). It was him—Mr. Ernest, your ladyship.

LADY BROCKLEHURST. With which lady?

LADY AGATHA (*rises*). I have already told you, Lady Brocklehurst, that Ernest and I—

LADY BROCKLEHURST. Yes, now, but you were two years on the island. (*To* TWEENY.) Was it this lady? (*Looking at* LADY MARY.)

TWEENY (*candidly*). No, your ladyship.

LADY BROCKLEHURST. Then I don't care which of the others it was. (TWEENY *giggles.*) Well, I suppose that will do.

(CRICHTON *bows and turns up, with* TWEENY. ALL *are relieved and relax a little.*)

LORD BROCKLEHURST. Do! I hope you are ashamed of yourself, Mother. (*Taking a pace in to* R.C.) Crichton. (CRICHTON *checks and comes down* C.) You are an excellent fellow, and if after we are married you ever wish to change your place, come to us.

LADY MARY (*rising*). Oh, no, impossible.

LADY BROCKLEHURST. Why impossible? (LADY MARY *cannot answer. To* CRICHTON.) Do you see why it should be impossible, my man?

(*General anxiety.*)

CRICHTON. Yes, my lady. (*They wonder. Turning towards* LORD LOAM, *who is up* C.) I had not told you, my lord, but as soon as your lordship is suited I wish to leave service.

LORD LOAM. Leave service?

CRICHTON. Yes, my lord.

TREHERNE. What will you do, Crichton?

(CRICHTON *shrugs his shoulders; "God knows," it may mean.* ALL *are relieved.*)

CRICHTON. Shall I withdraw, my lord?

(LORD LOAM *nods and turns away* L. CRICHTON *bows and withdraws without a tremor,* TWEENY *accompanying him. They can* ALL *breathe again; the thunder-storm is over.*)

LADY BROCKLEHURRST (*rising; thankful to have made herself unpleasant*). Horrid of me, wasn't it? (*She crosses* C.) But if one wasn't disagreeable now and again, it would be horribly tedious to be an old woman. (*Moving towards* LADY MARY.) He will soon be yours, Mary, and then—think of the opportunities you will have of being disagreeable to me. On that understanding, my dear, don't you think we might—?

(*Their cold lips meet.*)

LORD LOAM (*vaguely*). Quite so—quite so. (*He moves to* C.)

(CRICHTON *announces dinner.* LORD LOAM *gives* LADY BROCKLEHURST *his arm. The* OTHERS *file out.* LADY MARY *stays behind a moment and impulsively holds out her hand, meeting* CRICHTON *up* C.)

LADY MARY. To wish you every happiness.

CRICHTON (*an enigma to the last*). The same to you, my lady.

LADY MARY. Do you despise me, Crichton? (*The man who could never tell a lie makes no answer.*) You are the best man among us.

CRICHTON. On an island, my lady, perhaps—

LADY MARY. Tell me one thing; you have not lost your courage?

CRICHTON. No, my lady.

(LADY MARY exits. CRICHTON, impassive to the last, moves up and switches off the lights.)

CURTAIN.

THE ADMIRABLE CRICHTON

FURNITURE AND PROPERTY PLOT

Acts I and IV

Carpet on stage. Strip in hall.
Curtains at windows.
    On the Walls.—Oil paintings or good water-colours.
       Large oval mirror of the period (over the mantel).
    On the Mantel.—Large ornate clock.
       Some vases and good ornaments.
2 settees (R.C. and L.C.).
1 large armchair with high back (L.C.).
3 smaller armchairs (2 at R., 1 L. *of* R. settee).
3 other drawing-room chairs.
3 stools for drawing-room use.
1 low footstool or hassock.
1 oval table, for tea-tray, etc. (L.C.).
1 do. small (R.C.).
1 large bookcase, with glass doors and cupboard below.
1 china-cabinet (filled with porcelain ornaments, etc.).
1 corner cupboard (up R.).
1 floor standard lamp (R., above the fire).
1 or 2 small occasional tables, flowers stands, etc.
1 tall glass case (at L., for Act II, only).
    On the Table.—A large silver tray with cups and
      saucers, etc., and also plates, for about 18 persons,
      with milk jugs (2), sugar-bowls and 3 plates of
      cakes.
    Off Stage (up L.C.).—Tray with teapot, hot-water
    jug, etc.

PERSONAL

ERNEST.—Notes for speech.
LORD LOAM.—Notes for speech.
TOMPSETT.—Hat.

Act II

Grass on stage (short at c. acting area; long up stage
and either side).

Rock ledges, tropical bushes, etc., as in script.

Bucket (from the yacht, with name on it "BLUEBELL")
and board on the same, for a seat.

Tripod for fire. Stewing-pot with lid suspended at same.

Quantity of small twigs, branches, etc., for the fire.

Logs and rough planks for building the hut (at R.).

A cutlass, a hatchet, a thick stick, a hammer.

PERSONAL

ERNEST.—Paper and pencil.

CRICHTON.—Pipe, tobacco (some in each pocket). A
lens (small magnifier).

Act III

Stage cloth to represent wooden floor.

A few rough skins on floor as rugs.

> *On the Walls.*—Some animals' heads (tiger-cats,
> etc.) roughly mounted as trophies.
> Some rough weapons.

> *On the Joists.*—Cured hams, spades, etc.

Wood settee (R.C.).

Home-made dresser (at L.).

Rough wood table for 6 (L.C.).

8 or 9 rough wood stools, set as in the Ground Plan.

Chair (at c.), home made, or salvaged from the yacht.

2 small tables (1 at R. and 1 in the kitchen recess).

Wood plate-rack.

Sink (in kitchen).

Section of rowing-boat (as chimney).

Lever apparatus in wooden setting (as described for
"beacon").

Several plates, made from large shells.

2 or 3 knives.

Rough spoons and forks of wood and bone.
4 or 5 goblets or cups (home made, of wood).
2 or 3 jugs like the cups.
2 large wooden dishes.

PERSONAL

TWEENY.—Prop. armadillo bird for plucking. Cloth.
LORD LOAM.—Home-made concertina.
ERNEST.— 2 home-made buckets suspended on a "yoke" for carrying.

LADY AGATHA. } Fishing-rods. Large property fish,
LADY CATHERINE. } and canvas satchel with several small fishes.

LADY MARY.—Long bow and quiver of arrows. Prop. bird, and prop. buck. Wreath (on the dresser for the dinner scene).
CRICHTON.—Book.
TREHERNE.—Wooden box containing razors.
(NOTE.—Food to be provided as in script for the dinner scene.)

NOTE ON ACT IV

The chair above the fire is now against the R. wall.
The chair L. of the small table on the L. of the R. settee is pulled out a little.
The stool below the above small table is now set a little closer to the table, i. e., further up stage.
Between the windows L., is a large glass-case which is filled with curios from the island, and in the cupboard below is the bucket from the yacht.
There are other curios on the cabinet up C., suitably labelled.
On the walls are various weapons and stuffed birds, heads and skins.

LIGHTING PLOT

Act I

To Open.—Floats: Amber and pink ¾, white ½.
Battens: Amber and pink FULL; white ¾ (including batten over the hall).
Stage Floods: Off L., through the windows, straw; off L., into the hall, No. 7 pink and white, frost.
F. O. H.: Flood mingled straw, No. 7 pink and white, all frost.
Lengths: Amber on interior backing as required.
>*Cue.*—LORD LOAM. ". . . find me a valet who can do without three maids."—Commence slow check of L. floods to a half. Complete at exit of LORD LOAM.

Act II

To Open.—Floats: Amber and pink ½, white ¼.
Battens: Nos. 1 and 2, amber and pink FULL, white ½; No. 3 (and No. 4 if used) amber and blue only ¾.
F. O. H.: Flood straw and No. 7 pink, both frost.
Stage Floods: R. and L. (to kill shadows on cloth) straw. Ditto on upper section of cloth, No. 18 blue.
Perches: Straw if needed, or in place of F. O. H.
>NOTE.—These may be employed on hut, R.C., and rock L.C., acting areas.
Ground Rows: On each cloth and upstage foliage, amber ½.
>(NOTE.—If, instead of ordinary battens, a spot batten is used, these should be straw frost and No. 7 pink frost, mingled on R. and L.C., acting areas, and No. 7 pink only on R.C. area (tripod).
>*Cue* 1.—ERNEST. ". . . I'm planning the building of the hut."—Commence 10-minute check of amber

in floats to nil, and amber in battens to ½, **white** to nil. Bring in pink on ground row on cloth ½.

Cue 2.—TREHERNE. "Crichton is incapable of acting dishonourably."—Slow change of F. O. H. to No. 4 amber, frost, and No. 10 pink, frost. Check down stage floods by ½. Change flood on cloth **to** No. 20 blue.

Cue 3.—CRICHTON. ". . . without any interference from us."—Slowly check, amber in battens to nil, bringing in blue ½. Check down F. O. H. to ½. (Ditto for batten spots if used.) Blue floats ¼.

Cue 4.—ERNEST. ". . . forgetting this is an island."— Fade amber F. O. H. to nil, leaving only No. 10 pink frost at ½. Commence slow check of stage floods (except blues) to nil. Fade out amber in ground rows and bring in blues to ½. Batten on cloth change to blue only at ½. Bring in pink of c. section of floats up to ¾, fading out all circuits in R. and L. sections. When completed, bring in flood of moonlight blue up L. to catch fire area and lower side of hut, slowly.

Cue 5.—*When* CRICHTON *is left alone.*—Slightly check down all except moonlight blue and pink **in** c. section of floats.

ACT III

To Open.—Floats: Amber and pink ½, white ¼.

Battens: Amber and pink FULL, white ½ in Nos 1 and 2, and FULL in No. 3, over exterior.

Stage Floods (off L.): To flood exterior, No. 17 steel and straw frost.

F. O. H.: Flood straw, frost.

Lengths: Amber in interior backing up L.

Ground Row: On cloth, amber and pink ½.

Cue 1.—CRICHTON. "Clear, please."—Check white in floats to nil and in battens to ¼, slowly. Check F. O. H. down by ½.

Cue 2.—MARY. "If I could only please you, Gov."—

Check amber and pink in floats to ¼, and battens to ½. Slow fade out of steel flood on cloth, and white in No. 3 batten.

Cue 3.—CRICHTON. "No, by my side."—Commence to change flood on cloth to blue above and pink below, and fade amber in ground row. Change F. O. H. slowly to No. 4 amber frost.

Cue 4.—*As* CATHERINE *switches on.*—Up chandelier light, and bring up amber floats by ¼, and No. 1 batten by ½.

Cue 5.—*After* CRICHTON *switches on the "beacons."*— Change pink flood on cloth to orange, fading in to full in about one minute. When at ½, add red spot to flood lower section of cloth only, at ½. Then orange up to FULL. Follow with slight check of floats, and F. O. H. on c. acting area only (for CRICHTON *and* LADY MARY)

ACT IV

To Open.—Floats: Amber and pink ¾, blue ¼.

Battens: Amber and pink FULL, blue ¼, white ¼ (including the batten over the hall).

Stage Floods: Off L., through the windows, straw, frost; off L., into the hall, No. 7 pink and straw, frost.

F. O. H.: Flood mingled straw and No. 7 pink, frost (no white).

Lengths: Amber on interior backings as required.

Cue 1.—LADY MARY. "You have told *her!*"—Check amber and pink slowly in floats and battens by ¼, and change floods through windows to No. 4 amber very slowly. Follow with fade-out of white in battens to nil. Complete cue as LADY MARY exits after kiss.

Cue 2.—*After* CRICHTON *has announced* LADY BROCKLEHURST *he switches on the lights.*—Bring up amber and pink in floats to ¾ and in battens to FULL. No white. Blue unchanged. Change straw in F. O. H. to No. 52 gold.

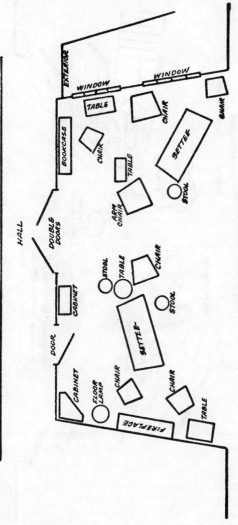

SCENE DESIGN — ACTS I & IV

"THE ADMIRABLE CRICHTON"

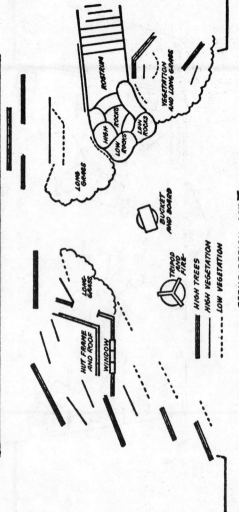

SEA & SKY BACKING

LONG GRASS

ROSTRUM

HIGH ROCKS

LOW ROCKS

LOW ROCKS

LOW ROCKS

VEGETATION AND LONG GRASS

LONG GRASS

HUT FRAME AND ROOF

WINDOW

BUCKET AND BOARD

TRIPOD AND FIRE.

HIGH TREES

HIGH VEGETATION

LOW VEGETATION

SCENE DESIGN—ACT II
"THE ADMIRABLE CRICHTON"